Meditation
Advice
to Beginners

Meditation
Advice to Beginners

Bokar Rinpoche

Translation from Tibetan into French
François Jacquemart

English Translation
Christiane Buchet

English Version Edited by
Jennifer Pessereau

Meditation
Advice to Beginners
by Bokar Rinpoche

Published by:
ClearPoint Press
PO Box 170658
San Francisco, CA 94117

The original text of this book was published in France and was entitled: La Méditation, conseils aux débutants.
Copyright reserved for all countries:
Editions Claire Lumière
Mas Vinsargues
13116 Vernègues, France.
Copyright © 1993 English Edition:
ClearPoint Press
Printed in the United States of America

Library of Congress Cataloging in Publication Data
Bokar Rinpoche
Meditation, Advice to Beginners
Includes Index
1. Tibetan Buddhism I. Title
2. Meditation
Library of Congress Catalogue Card Number: 92-075390
ISBN 0-9630371-1-0

Cover Design: Robin Spaan
Vajrasattva Cover Drawing: Cynthia Moku

INTRODUCTION

Meditation is currently a fashionable practice and there are already books published on this subject. Why this new book? What will you find in this volume? You will find teachings given by an authentic Tibetan teacher, Bokar Rinpoche. Not only does Bokar Rinpoche know meditation, but years of skillful practice allow him to guide students on this path. For him, Buddhism constitutes the essence of the spiritual domain and his teachings transmit the teachings given by the Buddha. Furthermore, they are perfectly adapted to our time and cultural environment. Bokar Rinpoche knows how to make clear that which, at first approach, seems obscure and complex. He really embodies the essence of these teachings. When one meets with Bokar Rinpoche, one is bathed in a radiant peace which he extends to all beings through his immense love and compassion. In his presence, one may experience a taste of the true nature of the mind. It is my hope that this book will convey to the reader Bokar Rinpoche's wisdom and compassion.

Since the series of teachings translated here come from public and private teachings given in France between 1985 and 1987, they sometimes address the people of a particular city. Their contents, however, are directed toward each of us, regardless of where we reside. You may sometimes find a repetition of themes from one chapter to another. We did not edit the teachings. As repetition may increase understanding, you will encounter the same view presented in a different context in some instances.

They are true teachings that one can read, put directly into practice, reread and practice again and again. For the person who wants to practice with others, there are many meditation centers throughout the world where one may receive instruction from a qualified teacher. This book is not a substitute for a living teacher but a guide to the path, a friendly companion on the journey sharing wisdom and experience.

Many familiar words, such as suffering, love and compassion, have a more specific meaning in the context of this book. To clarify their meaning, we have added a selective glossary of Buddhist terms in order to help the beginner more easily understand the text. This glossary is not exhaustive. Advanced students of Buddhism may refer to more scholarly publications for comprehensive definitions of these terms.

This book is the result of the love and efforts of many people. I am deeply grateful to Bokar Rinpoche who gave these simple but extraordinary teachings and to Lama Chöky (François Jacquemart) who translated them from Tibetan into French. In translating the book into English, I have had my work made easier by the generosity of a number of individuals. The following people have contributed substantially in the form of advice or assistance. Special thanks are due to Gene Meyer, Hubert Godard, Chiao and Ernie Crews for their love and support. Jacqueline Cattani read the first draft, corrected and checked the translation against the French. Don Iocca read the manuscript, and Dan Jorgensen helped with his computer expertise. Elson Snow shared his knowledge and art of printing. Françoise Buchet drew the illustrations pages 69, 108 and 112. Rosemary Gilpin helped in all the phases of this work, patiently rereading the text and offering encouragement and love.

May the reading of this book bring you much happiness!

The translator

TABLE OF CONTENTS

APPROACHING MEDITATION

General Introduction
to Meditation

Human beings are afflicted by suffering, anguish, and a number of fears which they are incapable of avoiding. The function of meditation is to eliminate this suffering and anguish.

We generally think that happiness and suffering come from external circumstances. Constantly preoccupied reorganizing the world, in one way or another, we try to rid ourselves of a little suffering here and accumulate a little happiness there, without ever obtaining the desired result. From the Buddhist point of view, as well as that of meditation, happiness and suffering do not fundamentally depend on the external circumstances, but on the mind itself. A positive mental attitude engenders happiness; a negative attitude produces suffering.

How can we understand this mistake which makes us look outside for that which we can only find inside? A person with a clean and clear face who looks in the mirror sees a clean, clear face. While a person whose face is dirty and covered with mud sees a dirty, mud-stained face. The reflection in the mirror has no true existence; only the face itself exists. Forgetting the face, we take its reflection as real. The positive or negative nature of our mind is reflected in outward appearances which reflect back our own image. This external manifestation is an echo of the quality of our inner world. The happiness that we hope for will not come from restructuring the world which surrounds us but from reforming the one within.

The unwanted suffering will cease, only if we do not tarnish our mind with negativity. As long as we do not recognize that both happiness and suffering have their source within our own mind, and do not know how to distinguish between that which is helpful or harmful for our mind, allowing it to remain in its ordinary unhealthiness, we remain powerless to establish a state of genuine happiness. We would be powerless to avoid continual reappearance of suffering. Whatever our hopes, we will always be disappointed.

If we discover in the mirror's reflection that our face is dirty and begin to wash the mirror, we can scrub it for years, but it will not make a difference. Not the smallest amount of dirt nor the tiniest stain will disappear from our reflection. Because our efforts are not directed toward the right object, they will be totally in vain. This is one of the first principles of Buddhism and meditation: the understanding that happiness and suffering do not fundamentally depend on the external world but upon our own mind. If we do not understand this, we will never turn inward, and will continue in vain to base our energies and hopes on external pursuits. Understanding, we can wash our face, and thus the reflection will appear clean in the mirror.

HELPFUL CONDITIONS FOR MEDITATION

Meditation concerns the mind. However, effective meditation requires a number of helpful conditions without which our efforts would not be fruitful.

First, after having understood that happiness and suffering essentially depend on our mind, we must have an intense *aspiration* to meditate and feel *joy* at the prospect.

Second, guidance by an *instructor* who teaches how to meditate is necessary. If we decided to go somewhere in an uncharted region without the help of a guide, we might not reach our destination. Left to chance, we would only get lost or take very long detours. In a similar way, without a master to guide our meditation, we would only get lost on crisscrossing paths.

Third, the *place* where we meditate is important, particularly for beginners. The circumstances in which we are living actually exert a very constraining influence upon us and encourage a profusion of thoughts that paralyze our attempts to meditate. Therefore, retiring to a place removed to some extent from mundane activities is necessary. A wild animal living in the high mountain forest cannot endure the agitation of the city. In the same manner, the meditative mind cannot develop in conditions where continuous, external distractions and temptations reign.

HOW TO MEDITATE

Once we have set ourselves in an isolated place, we must free our body from all external activity, free our mind from thoughts concerning the past and future, and free our speech from profane conversation. Our body, speech and mind can then rest in a state of *natural ease*.

Bodily posture is important. Our body is covered by a network of *subtle channels* (*nadis*) in which circulate the *subtle winds*[1] (*prana*). The production of thoughts is linked with the circulation of these *winds*. The agitation of the body causes the agitation of the *channels* and *winds* which in turn induce mental turbulence.

Activity of speech, the formation of sounds, also depends on the activity of the *winds*. Talking too much disturbs them and increases the production of thoughts, while remaining silent aids the meditation.

In this way, tranquility of speech and body creates the conditions for inner calm by avoiding the production of excessive thoughts. Just as a rider is at ease when he or she handles his or her mount well, the mind will rest when body and speech are under control.

There are some false notions concerning meditation. For some people, meditation is reviewing and analyzing the events of daily life and of the past days, months and years. For others, meditation means considering the future, reflecting on how to act or planning long or short-term projects. These two approaches are both in error. Production of thoughts about the past or future is in itself contradictory to the establishment of mental calm even if the body and speech remain inactive. As far as an exercise does not lead to inner peace, it is not meditation.

Those who do not chase after the past or future may instead settle into a vague and blurred state close to numbness which induces great fatigue. The mind dwells in an obscure indetermination which may seem positive because the mind appears to be contented and at rest. However, this state lacks lucidity entirely and may encourage one to slip into drowsiness which is then averted only by the emergence of a flood of uncontrolled thoughts.

---

[1]The *subtle winds* or *subtle energies* are the link between the mind and the body.

True meditation avoids these pitfalls. The mind is not preoccupied with the past, does not consider the future, but is settled in the present in a lucid, clear, and calm state. Our mind can be compared to the sea. At night we can only perceive the sea obscurely. However, during the day we can see precisely every detail of color, wave, foam, rocks, and depth. Ultimately we should be as clearly conscious of our inner situation, as we are of the sea during the day. If the mind is allowed to relax, like waves it naturally calms down. This is the inner calm, technically called mental calming or, in Tibetan, *shinay*.

Shinay can be developed by many methods. For example, a beginner can visualize a small sphere of white light at the level of the forehead and concentrate on that to the best of one's abilities. One can also concentrate on the inhaling and exhaling of breath or can rest the mind in a state of non-distraction without taking any particular object of concentration. Employing any of these three methods will aid in learning to meditate.

Furthermore, it is important to approach each session of meditation with a spacious, open mind. One should not fixate on the hope that the meditation will be good or the fear that it will not be good. The mind should be relaxed, free and vast. The meditator should be free of the hindrances of hoping for a good meditation or fearing a bad one.

Sometimes during meditation we experience happiness and peace. Satisfied, we rejoice at having had a good meditation. Sometimes, on the other hand, our mind is disturbed by many thoughts during the session, and sadly, we may judge ourselves to be poor meditators. Rejoicing in a good meditation and being attached to pleasant experiences as well as being unhappy about a bad meditation are both inappropriate attitudes. Whether the meditation is good or bad does not matter; the important thing is simply to meditate.

Early on in meditation, some beginners may have good experiences to which they become attached and which they expect to constantly repeat. When this does not happen, they become disappointed and may even give up meditation. On a long journey sometimes we travel on the right roads, sometimes on the wrong ones. If the charm of an agreeable part of the journey causes us to continually stop and delight in it or if the difficulties of the wrong road cause us to give up going further, we will never reach our destination. Whether the road be right or wrong, we must persevere without worrying about the difficulties or becoming attached to pleasant moments.

Beginners should limit themselves to short sessions of ten or fifteen minutes. Even if meditation is going well, one should stop. Then, if there is enough time, one may have a second short session after a pause. It is better to proceed with a series of short sessions than to engage oneself in a long session. Even if a longer session begins well, the novice meditator risks falling into difficulties or becoming tired.

FRUITS OF MEDITATION

At the beginning our mind is not able to remain stable and rest for very long. However, with perseverance and consistency, calm and stability gradually develop. We also feel a greater sense of physical and inner ease. In addition, the strong hold of fortunate or unfortunate external circumstances—which is initially very powerful— begins to decrease and we find ourselves less enslaved by them. Deepening our experience of the true nature of the mind in effect decreases the influence of the outer world upon us and strengthens us.

The ultimate fruit of meditation is the attainment of Perfect Awakening, or Buddhahood. At this point one is totally liberated from the cycle of conditioned existence and from the suffering that creates it. At the same time one has the power to effectively help others.

The path of meditation is divided into two stages. The first is called *shinay* (mental calming) in which we gradually quiet our inner agitation. The second is called *lhatong* (superior vision) which leads to elimination of ego clinging which is the basis of the cycle of existence. Only the inner path leads to Awakening. No substance or external invention has this power.

CONCLUSION

Engaging in the path of meditation demands that one know its aim, the means employed and the results one can obtain:

• recognize that the source of all suffering and all happiness is the mind itself; consequently, only training the mind allows us to eliminate suffering and establish genuine and lasting happiness.

• know the necessary supporting conditions: the wish to meditate, a qualified instructor, and a secluded place.

• know how to establish the mind in meditation: without following thoughts about the past or future, keep the mind in the present in an open, relaxed and lucid state while placing it on the chosen object of concentration.

• know the provisional and ultimate fruits of meditation: serenity, freedom in the face of circumstances, and finally, Buddhahood.

Question: Can one meditate while working?

Answer: If we work without distraction, mindful of what we are doing, this is also meditation.

Question: At the beginning how long should one meditate and with what frequency? Can one meditate with closed eyes?

Answer: If one does not have much time, regularly meditating, even fifteen minutes a day, is immediately beneficial. If one has more time, two fifteen-minute sessions are better. Keeping the eyes open or closed depends on which is helpful to you. When the mind is agitated by many thoughts, closing the eyes may be beneficial. If this is not the case, one may keep the eyes open. Apart from the relationship with our thoughts, this does not have much importance.

Question: Are there any risks in meditation?

Answer: If one trusts oneself to a qualified instructor, there are none. If, on the other hand, one meditates without guidance, one's meditation may be sterile or one may, in fact, be at risk.

Question: In some meditations, one uses symbols of the five elements with specific colors. Is this merely a convention or is there some deep reason for it?

Answer: The mode of being of the mind includes the ultimate nature of these five elements. When this is realized, the essential nature of the five elements is recognized as being the five female Buddhas. Without realization, the five ordinary elements appear. The colors attributed to the five elements are those of their primordial nature. Therefore, this is not merely a convention.

Question: Once thoughts are quieted, how can one avoid staying in a blank tranquility?

Answer: To avoid the lack of clarity or becoming sleepy, one must increase one's vigilance. However, vigilance should be judiciously regulated. If it is too tight, additional thoughts will be generated; if it is too loose, the result will be sleepiness or stupor. The right balance is necessary.

Question: At a certain point in your talk, I heard the phrase "neither joy nor sorrow" which would imply a state of emotional neutrality. In these conditions, what does the "redirection of self for the benefit of others" mean?

Answer: It is true that meditation frees us from external joy and suffering. However, when one meditates, one develops the thoughts of obtaining Awakening for the benefit of **all** beings. The result of this orientation generated in one's mind will be that, once Awakening is attained, one will spontaneously benefit the universe without either effort or partiality. The sun shares its beneficial radiance with all beings and all manifestation, without thinking: "I have to warm such and such, I must ripen this fruit, and so on." Similarly, the beneficial radiance of the Buddhas is spontaneously extended to all beings. This radiance is, however, not unconscious. Buddhas are fully conscious of the situation of beings and their own action. They know the distress of those they help, yet their action is effortless. This activity is expressed in the domain of manifestation in different ways. The Body of Perfect Experience[1] guides already pure beings. The Body of Emanation is addressed to ordinary beings like ourselves, as are sacred supports such as statues, paintings, *mantras*, and so on.

Question: Can one achieve realization through reading texts alone?

Answer: Without a qualified teacher, the texts are not sufficient. That which we read in texts does not leave a deep enough imprint on our mind. On the other hand, that which we receive from the lips of a master makes a sufficiently deep imprint and engenders strong confidence.

Question: What bothers me about meditation is the word

---

[1]The plenitude of Buddhahood, which is another means of defining Awakening is described in terms of the Three Bodies of a Buddha. In this context, "Body" does not mean physical organism; rather, it is an aspect of being.

- The *Absolute Body* (Sanskrit, *Dharmakaya*), called literally "Ultimate Body of All Existence," is unmanifested, impossible to conceive with any amount of determination, ineffable, and similar to space. Though it can be called eternal, infinite or nontemporal and non-spacial, the play of all time and space is contained within it.

- The *Body of Perfect Experience* (Sanskrit, *Sambhogakaya*) called the Body of Complete Enjoyment of the Qualities of Awakening, is a formal manifestation of Awakening. It is non-material and of the nature of the light which emanates from the dynamic of the Absolute Body. Though it is invisible to ordinary beings, it can be perceived by *Bodhisattvas* of the three superior levels. Because it is not of the transitory nature of phenomena, it is not subject to temporal change.

- The *Body of Emanation* (Sanskrit, *Nirmanakaya*) refers to a Buddha appearing within the sphere of ordinary manifestation such as the Buddha Sakyamuni. Being the expression of compassion, he or she guides beings toward liberation.

Often a fourth Body is added—the *Body of Essence Itself* (Sanskrit, *Svabhavikakaya*)—which actually expresses the indivisibility of the other three Bodies.

"method." A method is something which organizes, conditions and orients the mind. I wonder how one can attain something which is unconditional and unoriented with these methods. Our knowledge, thoughts, and emotions are the result of time. What also bothers me in these methods is that one uses time. However, liberating oneself from any constraint is also liberating oneself from time.

Answer: Once the ultimate nature of the mind is realized, there is no longer any need of methods. However to realize the state beyond method, one must rely on them. Without this support, it is impossible to realize the ultimate state. The methods do imply a progression contained within a time frame. However, it is by relying on time that one attains the timeless.

Question: Does time really exists, or is it only a projection of the mind?

Answer: From the ultimate point of view, Buddhahood, there is no time. Nevertheless, time does exist for us until we attain ultimate realization. Now we perceive the three times—past, present, and future—as real. Considering the past or future to be real creates much suffering because of the many memories, worries and projects that agitate our mind. In fact, the past does not exist anymore and the future does not exist yet, but we suffer because we make these two illusory concepts real through thinking. Among the three times, the past and future cause us the most suffering even though they do not exist. And within this domain, the future prevails over the past. We now conceive that these three times really exist. Through a progression in time spent meditating, we gradually deepen our understanding of the lack of reality of the three times until we eventually arrive at the timeless.

Question: Since things are impermanent, does that suggest that time exists?

Answer: Time exists for us now and consequently impermanence. Timelessness is eternity.

More to Consider

Many people wish to meditate. They understand that meditation concerns the mind but generally they do not know precisely what meditation is.

It is a little like our concept of the sky. Everyone knows what the sky is, no one will ever tell you, "The sky? I do not know what it is." But the idea one has of the sky is very imprecise and it is rare to meet someone able to define it. If you ask, "What is the sky?," the person questioned will only point the finger up and say, "That is the sky." Similarly for meditation: one knows it exists, often one thinks it is good but one does not really know what it is.

What *is* the sky?

One will usually say that the sun is in the center of the sky, the notion of center implying that of borders. A person would be inclined to conceive the center and borders in relation to a country but a resident of another country would apply the same relation to his or her country. This is sufficient to show that the sky's center and borders are only subjective notions and are not a complete description of the reality.

People who have the good fortune to live in Provence often say, "How beautiful the sky is here." Is it therefore possible to delimit a piece of the sky about which one could say in an exclusive manner, "This part of the sky is the sky of Provence."

Everyone also knows that the sky is blue, but few people know why. Where does it come from? Is it material? Nonmaterial? And how large is it?

Meditation concerns the mind. The mind is very similar to the sky: without form, without substance and without dimension. As for the sky, everyone knows it exists but few are those who know what it really is. Like the sky, the mind is without center and limit. We do not yet have the experience of this unlimited state; on the contrary, we reduce the infinite to the finite and stay locked up in the narrow confines of what we call "I." The reduction corresponds to the subjective limitation implied in the notion of "our sky" when a person from Provence, for instance, talks about the sky as if one could cut out a piece of it and define it as specifically related to one region. Within the infinite mind, without center or limit, we identify ourselves with a very reduced entity: the ego. From this, all of our physical as well as mental suffering and difficulties arise.

It is true that certain types of suffering are related to external circumstances and that it is almost possible to find material solutions. When facing internal suffering, on the other hand, material solutions will not be effective.

Let us imagine a king in a peaceful and flourishing country, well guarded in his palace, at night. This king who possesses all the external circumstances of happiness, is sleeping. In his dream, an enemy appears who pursues and seeks to kill him. The king suffers anxiety and fear. The suffering of this dream would not be relieved by any remedy outside the mind of the dreamer. We can similarly possess all the material conditions necessary to be happy but this is of no help to the mind which suffers. Only the spiritual path and meditation will allow us to be freed from inner suffering, anxiety and difficulties.

EGO AND THE FIVE POISONS

Our mind is fundamentally infinite. It is not limited by the constraints of an individual existence. There is no ego. Although it does not exist, we identify ourselves with this illusory ego. It is the center and the touchstone of all our relationships. Everything that confirms its existence and is favorable to it becomes an object of *attachment*. Everything that threatens its integrity becomes an enemy, a source of *aversion*. The presence of the ego itself conceals the true nature of our mind and of phenomena. It makes us unable to discriminate between the real and the illusory. In this sense, we are prisoners of *mental dullness*. The ego also engenders *jealousy* toward persons considered possible rivals in any possible area. Finally the ego wants to be superior to others. This is *pride*.

Attachment, aversion, mental dullness, jealousy, and pride are the five basic poisons produced by ego clinging.

They form irrevocable obstacles to inner peace, constantly creating worries, troubles, difficulties, anguish and suffering, not only for ourselves but also for others. It is obvious, for example, that anger results in suffering for oneself and when overcome by an opponent, curses and hurtful words, for the person toward whom it is directed.

Likewise, ego and the five poisons lead us to harm ourselves and others which leave imprints with negative karmic[1] potential on our mind. The ripening of this karmic potential will be expressed in the form of future painful circumstances.

---

[1] The *law of karma*, which means literally *law of cause and effect*, states that any act accomplished within the duality of a subject and object, whether the act is physical, verbal or mental, carries an effect back to the one who acts. This effect is at first completely invisible and imperceptible, similar to an imprint or a seed which would be planted in the more subtle layers of an individual's consciousness (even more subtle than the unconscious described by the psychoanalysts) in the *alayavijnana*, the reservoir or potential of consciousness. Starting from this latent state, a process of ripening begins which generally spreads over several lifetimes, indeed hundreds of lifetimes, at the end of which the karmic seed would be expressed, determining either the general circumstances of an existence (sex, nationality, wealth, physical, intellectual and emotional possibilities, and so forth), or the temporary conditions (an illness, an encounter, a success, a failure, and so on). Everything works, for example, like a computer: the numerous data interact with each other and with the new data continually added, modifying the results more or less. Since we constantly act under the conditions of duality, a defective approach cast only aside with Awakening, there is a permanent flood of new elements nourishing our karmic potential at the same time as a constant ripening gets rid of older impressions. The whole process, far from being static, is constantly moving. One should be reminded not to forget that all phenomena which regulate our life are the expression of our *karma*; isolating one element is a frequent mistake. It is a completely fragmentary conception thinking that, for instance, if one is sick, it is a karmic result and therefore it is not useful to seek medical care. We forget that our *karma* includes an existence of physicians and hospitals to whom we can go for help.

The law of *karma* is, in fact, a very large view of the physical laws that regulate our universe. If one sows wheat, it will not grow into rice. Randomness does not prevail in the matter, no more than it operates in the conditions of existence of individuals. Very complex and dependent upon the interaction of infinite elements, karmic causality can be summarized, however, in a very simple principle: whoever creates suffering, implants in their own inmost depths, the potential for suffering: whoever creates happiness implants the potential for happiness.

- 18 -

The ego and its entourage are our true enemy—not a visible enemy which can be defeated by weapons or material objects—but an invisible enemy which can only be defeated by meditation and following a spiritual path. Contemporary science has developed extremely powerful weapons, bombs that can kill hundreds of thousands of people. However, no bomb can annihilate the ego and the five poisons. In this domain the true atomic bomb is meditation.

THE MIND ON VACATION

Our mind in its usual state, is constantly occupied by thoughts tied to the five poisons. They come one after another, sometimes under the influence of aversion, sometimes attachment, sometimes mental dullness, sometimes jealousy and sometimes pride. The intensity of these thoughts can vary greatly but there is not an instant when our mind is not agitated by them.

It is a beautiful day of vacation: no work to do, food is ready, no discussion to undertake. We can be seated quietly without any outer worries, however, our mind tires. Continually disturbed, even slightly, by the play of the poisons that occupy it, it is unable to establish itself in genuine peace. The mind is not on vacation. The mind can only take a vacation through meditation. Not because meditation permits the total disappearance of the thoughts but because they lose some of their strength and the contours become blurred for intervals. When this happens, the mind knows increased peace and happiness. It rests.

Westerners work in an office or elsewhere, and have some vacation time each year. They use the occasion to go to foreign countries, perhaps, or to the seashore, the mountains or the countryside, with the intention of finding happiness and rest. Unfortunately, the mind itself does not go on vacation: the five poisons, suffering and inner difficulties are part of the journey. In fact, it is only half a vacation. Only meditation provides a full vacation.

MEDITATION IN DAILY LIFE

A beginner should retire to a calm place, adopt a specific posture, remain silent and respect certain conditions. Through habit and experience, however, one becomes able to meditate in all circumstances: while walking, working, talking, eating, and so on. When one reaches that point, one has a lot of time for meditation. Furthermore, in all circumstances one can maintain a serene, open and relaxed mind. This experience of ease and serenity is itself meditation.

It is also an experience of freedom. Freedom is a value to which people attach an extreme importance nowadays. We could have all kinds of external freedom, but as long as our mind remains prisoner of its poisons and thoughts, we will not be free.

An inexperienced driver is very tense while driving; he or she is afraid of having an accident, or not knowing how to operate the vehicle properly. When the driver becomes accustomed to driving, he or she can talk with the person seated at his or her side while being completely present in what he or she does. The conversation does not prevent him or her from concentrating on handling the car or being attentive to the road signs. The inexperienced meditator should, in a similar way, be attentive only to the exercise of meditation. Progressively, he or she will develop the ability to pursue meditation while doing something else, like talking or working. One feels then a great sense of ease and genuine freedom on any occasion.

As we progress in meditative practice, the poisons of the mind become less virulent and our thoughts decrease. Even when they remain present, they lose their compelling character, and are no longer causes for suffering. Our mind calms down and knows joy. This latter reflects even on our physical appearance: our face becomes open, welcoming and joyful. We become easy to approach and pleasant. Others like to see us frequently. Inner peace and happiness radiate toward the outer world.

SUBJECTIVITY

Our manner of perceiving beings and the world principally depends on our state of mind. Suppose that you are invited to dinner by a person toward whom you feel deep hatred. The place is agreeable, the food is good, however, your hatred makes the food taste awful and the place lack charm. When on the other hand, a person that you cherish invites you to a place without charm and serves you a mediocre meal, the dishes become exquisite and the environment a paradise!

The difference is created by our mode of perception, which is conditioned by our attachment or aversion.

MEDITATION: ALREADY PRESENT IN US

Meditation is not something that a Buddha or a spiritual teacher can insert into our mind from outside. It is already present although only as a potential state. A teacher can only point out this latent presence and provide the means to discover it in ourselves. We all possess the state of meditation but we do not know how to use it. We are in the situation of someone who possesses a beautiful car but does not know how to drive. The car, as perfect as it may be, cannot go anywhere. However, one can find an instructor and learn how to drive. One may need one or two months of instruction, at the end of which our efforts directed by the instructor will allow us to use the car which has been unusable until now. Similarly, the state of meditation and Buddhahood are already present within us but without the help of a qualified instructor, we are unable to make them operational. It would be strange to possess an excellent car, and to have to leave it in the garage simply because one would not learn to drive. It is equally strange to allow the potential for awakening our mind to remain dormant simply because we are unwilling to make the effort and lack the perseverance required to learn to meditate.

PERSEVERANCE

To go from Aix-en-Provence to Paris[1] by car is a long way. Having never made this journey, we might think, perhaps, that one hour would be enough. In fact, after one hour on the road, we have to recognize that there are still many miles to drive. If this perspective discourages us and we prefer to stop where we are, we will never arrive in Paris.

Similarly, certain people engage in meditation full of hope. If after some months (indeed even some days) of assiduous practice, they do not achieve the results they hope, they get bored and give up. A long trip by car is tiring. This is why one breaks it up by pausing to drink

---

[1]Translator's note: it is approximately five hundred miles.

some tea or coffee. When weariness affects one's meditation, rather than give up in frustration or disinterest, one takes a break to relax the mind, and then engages on the path again.

Beginners have a general appreciation for meditation but find it difficult to sustain the effort. They are confident in the path, they have the necessary intelligence to understand it, but often lack the essential diligence and perseverance.

Initial attempts at meditation are often mixed with grand hopes to rapidly obtain extraordinary inner experiences. This expectation is dashed: not so many wonderful experiences, no extraordinary states. We are in a hurry but the inner world does not heed our impatience. Discouraged, we try another path, which in its turn lets us down, then we try another and still another.

How can one progress under these conditions?

Let us imagine that you wish to grow a flower: you prepare the soil, you sow the seed, water it, and feed it with fertilizer. Soon a shoot appears which does not have anything in common with the beauty of the flower you are trying to grow. Disappointed, you pull out the plant and thinking to do better, you sow another seed. Inevitably, the result will be the same. You may sow as many seeds as you want, but you will never see the flower. Patience and constant care of the plant are necessary for the flower to bloom some day. Meditation also requires time before it will be fruitful. Patience, perseverance and regularity will bring forth the blossom of the splendid flower of the mind one day. Meditating, even if only ten minutes a day without fail, is already beneficial. In a month, one would have meditated five hours. Continuing like this regularly during many months and years, would certainly allow one to progress.

Understanding the benefits of meditation is not possible without personal experience, as impossible as comprehending the taste of an unknown food. If, never having tasted chocolate, you ask me to explain its flavor to you, I could tell you:
- H'm, it is good!
- How good?
- Well, it is sweet.
- How sweet?

By bringing together facts, perhaps I will be successful in giving you a very approximate idea of chocolate. It will, however, remain something more or less mysterious. If, on the other hand, you put a piece of chocolate in your mouth, you will know immediately the flavor, without any possible hesitation. An explanation, even detailed, of the benefits of meditation will always remain unable to convey an understanding of them. Only personal practice and direct experience will allow you to discover its genuine taste.

QUESTIONS AND ANSWERS

Question: I have meditated for several years but I now have the feeling that I am regressing.

Answer: This can come from *karma* or from the fact that you are investing less effort and diligence in your practice. This feeling of regression is often a sign of letting go, of lack of energy. But it could also be a mistake in your way of meditating.

When we meet difficulties in meditation, we should apply some remedies. To provide support for what is properly called meditation, one must practice techniques to purify oneself, gather merit, open oneself to the grace of the spiritual teacher, and develop aspiration and diligence. In order for a flower to appear, it is not sufficient to have a seed, it must be nourished by soil, water, fertilizer and warmth. Meditation also requires supporting conditions: purification, merit, grace, frequently listening to instructions, effort, and perseverance. Only meditation in its complete context leads to Awakening.

It sometimes happens that, even when one is progressing, one has the feeling of stagnation; or stagnating, one feels one is making progress! We are often poor judges of our own meditation.

Question: Are Westerners handicapped in their efforts to meditate by their mental complexity?

Answer: Differences and difficulties probably do not come from the complexity of people's minds. It is true that in India or Tibet, conditions of life have been simpler but the people's minds are also complex, obstructed by all kinds of thoughts and preoccupations. Westerners cultivate much more their intellectual faculties than Easterners, to the detriment of spiritual values. Easterners, on their part, have much greater faith and diligence. This is without doubt the true difference.

Question: Is Buddhahood only peace of mind, or does it imply also particular knowledge?

Answer: Infinite peace of mind is a Buddha's own destiny. Inherent in this peace are revealed qualities which are expressed for the benefit of others. A Buddha possesses total knowledge of the ultimate nature of all phenomena. He or she sees simultaneously that ordinary beings, deprived of this knowledge, suffer. From then on, he or she is love and compassion made effective and activated through his or her power to benefit others.

Question: Could you give us a comparison to help us understand illusion?

Answer: We take appearances for real. Meditation leads us to an understanding of the illusory characteristics of these appearances: they are similar to a reflection in a mirror. In a like manner, the illusory nature of sound is perceived to be similar to an echo. Our thoughts, erroneously accepted as something real, are in fact like a mirage. Giving a real, inherent existence to appearances, sounds and thoughts creates suffering. Perceiving the unreality of appearances, sounds and thoughts does not mean cessation of manifestation but it denotes an understanding that any manifestation is lacking intrinsic reality. At the same time, it loses all power to engender suffering.

Fertile Ground

Among all the possibilities of existence, human existence occupies a privileged place[1]; moreover, Western countries are currently enjoying particularly good material conditions of life. This has not come about through random chance. Similar to that of the gods, it is from a karmic[2] point of view, the result of positive past activity, or more specifically the practice of giving.

However, these fortunate outer circumstances do not escape the domain of conditioned existence, and are therefore transitory and changing by nature. If we have not discovered the inner peace of the ultimate truth, these external elements are still insufficient to grant us genuine happiness. Many Westerners are conscious of this now. Wanting to discover this inner reality, they are turning

---

[1]Buddhism considers numerous possibilities of existence in addition to that of human beings and animals. In some existences, there is greater happiness than in the human realm, as, for instance, in the world of gods or *devas*, which will be discussed later. In others, there is suffering beyond what we can imagine on earth. The totality of these existences constitutes "conditioned existence" or what is called *samsara*, the wheel of existence. Getting out of the cycle of rebirths and suffering, is "liberation."

[2]See page 18

toward the *dharma*[1]. It is meditation that makes this discovery possible. If we learn the art of meditation sufficiently well, the importance and significance of meditation are measured in the three following results:

• through meditation, all suffering can be transformed into happiness;

• through meditation, the conflicting emotions which agitate our mind can be transformed into primordial, non-dual knowledge;

• through meditation, *samsara* can be transformed into *nirvana*, or, that is, the ordinary world is transformed into awakened reality.

However, meditating implies that one knows the method which allows one to do it correctly. It is not sufficient to tell oneself: "I am going to meditate," and to remain in some kind of undefined state.

INCLUDING ONESELF IN A TRADITION

Meditation is part of a set of practices called a spiritual tradition. The one which we are studying goes back to the Buddha whose teachings are the foundation, and it has been transmitted to us by a succession of teachers.

In this tradition, the path of meditation begins with the trust one has in the person who initiated it. This trust

---

[1]The term *dharma* signifies the spiritual path in general or the path taught by the Buddha, depending on the context.

is expressed by the act of *taking Refuge*[1] through which one places oneself under the spiritual influence of the Buddha. We understand that the Buddha can help us when we recognize the greatness of the Buddha's qualities which are summarized as three principal ones: infinite wisdom, infinite love, and infinite power to help beings. It is, therefore, with joy and respect that we place ourselves under the Buddha's protection and trust.

Without this trust placed in the Buddha, we will necessarily lack trust in the teachings, and we will not be able to meditate according to the instructions. On the other hand, trust in the teachings will naturally follow trust in the Buddha, and from this the conviction of the validity of the instructions for meditation. Learning to meditate thus, we will not encounter any obstacle.

UNDERSTANDING OUR SITUATION

On the foundation of this trust, it is useful to understand our situation. It is not at all without cause. If we now experience a certain happiness, it is the result of positive behavior in our past lives. On the other hand, our suffering is caused by past negative activity. Future happiness will be similarly based on our present positive behavior, and future suffering on our negative behavior. This is one of the essential points of Buddhism. One who understands the relation between cause and effect well, who grasps the long term relationship between that which is done and that which is experienced, will spontaneously

---

[1]*Taking Refuge* is the act by which one places oneself under the spiritual influence of the Buddha, the teachings and the community of realized beings. It is, for the first time, a brief ceremony, then a thought that one renews, following the tradition, at the beginning of each meditation.

be led to give up any negative activity, and to adopt a more correct behavior, which will moreover establish a certain inner and natural peace. Conflicting thoughts and emotions, as well as the suffering they cause, will lose their grasp on one's mind, and meditation itself will be easier.

We must, on the other hand, understand that our aspiration and that of all beings is similar. Each of us wishes for happiness. This desire for happiness is exactly the same for all beings. In the same manner that we never wish to suffer, similarly, no being wishes to suffer. Through this understanding, anger, aggression and malevolence will naturally be erased from our mind, and we will develop love, compassion and kindness. We will then certainly be able to begin to meditate fruitfully.

FERTILE GROUND

It is necessary to thoroughly understand the importance of the foundations thus laid out. If you attempt to grow a flower or a tree in stony ground or in sterile soil, you will not succeed. If, on the other hand, you prepare the soil, remove the stones, and add rich fertilizer, your seeds and plants will grow easily and vigorously. Soon, you will obtain flowers. Similarly, if we have not done the groundwork carefully by correcting our behavior and by engendering love and compassion within ourselves, our meditation will not develop. The soil is fertile, meditation will blossom without difficulties.

DISTRACTION

Our mind is continually attracted to objects that our senses capture: forms seen by the eyes, sounds heard by the ears, smells, tastes and tactile sensations. Not only is the mind occupied by these objects but, in the relationship it establishes with them, it superposes on them notions that it creates. It perceives certain objects as agreeable and develops attachment toward them. It interprets others as disagreeable and conceives aversion for them. Attachment and aversion, in their turn, cause suffering in the mind that produces them.

Sometimes our mind is not distracted by objects of senses; neither forms, sounds, smells, tastes, nor touch occupy the mind. However, it is not at rest because it is occupied by a stream of thoughts that continues without interruption and takes over all its energy. Thus, it does not know any peace.

Several of these thoughts refer to that which we have experienced in the past, maybe the same day, the day before, the previous week or month, or even several years before. More often even, our mind projects itself into the future: we anticipate the events which will occur tomorrow, next week or next month, unless of course we are in the process of analyzing our present state. In brief, whether our speculations are on the past, present or future, they do not cease. In fact, suffering is created by clinging to the belief that our thoughts are something real.

Distracted by sense objects or by the succession of thoughts, our mind never remains stable in its own essence. Knowing how to maintain one's mind in its own essence, as it is, without being distracted by either outer phenomena or inner thoughts, is precisely what we mean by meditation.

TAKING AN OBJECT

For a beginner, meditating is not without difficulties because the mind has the tendency to follow its natural inclinations and habits. Therefore, it is advised—to the degree it is possible—to meditate in a secluded place which allows one to avoid some sources of outer distractions. However, to find a place totally free of distractions, one would have to establish oneself on the side of a high mountain, and not have to relate to anyone. This risks being unrealistic if you have a family, children, a job, and so on. One could say to oneself, "Well my situation is that I live in a city! Better cross meditation out." This is not at all true, because even in the city, one can meditate.

In effect, while one is learning to meditate, it is often very difficult to place the mind in its own essence, and so one uses supports to guide it to inner calm. Any external object can be used: a glass, a table, a light, a statue of the Buddha, or any object that pleases us. One then directs all one's attention on the object, without distraction. It is simple attention which implies neither analysis nor commentary. If, for instance, one concentrates on a glass such as this one (*Bokar Rinpoche shows a glass placed on the table in front of him during the teaching*), one does not examine its form, note its characteristic, nor evaluate its qualities no more than one asks whether it contains liquid. The mind is simply placed on the glass, without distraction and without talking.

If, during this exercise, the appearance of the glass is clear and precise, it is a sign that our mind is truly concentrated. If, on the other hand, the glass becomes blurred and imprecise in appearance, it is a sign that our mind is being carried away by other thoughts.

When done regularly, this exercise, whatever the chosen object, will bring great benefit.

If you live in the city, you will find yourselves in the midst of many noises: cars, machines and so on—all the things one thinks will prevent oneself from meditating. If rather than considering these noises as obstacles, you take them as the object itself of your attention, they can become the support of your meditation. In this case, whether it is a loud or soft noise, agreeable or disagreeable, does not make any difference. Here again you can easily verify the quality of your attention: if the sounds are perceived precisely and without interruption, this is a sign of good attention. A discontinuous and vague perception will reveal the insufficiency of your attention.

One can proceed in the same manner with other sensory objects: smells, tastes, and contacts. It is also true that we can learn to meditate wherever we are, without it being necessary to leave anything. To retire to a mountain achieves nothing more than isolating ourselves from objects which provoke distraction. If we can meditate using these same objects as supports, it serves the same purpose.

MEDITATING ON THE MIND

By regularly concentrating like this on objects, we are preparing ourselves to meditate on the mind.

We have seen how our mind has always been occupied by a continual stream of thoughts, mainly about the past and the future. A little reflection, however, allows us to become conscious, first, of the uselessness of thoughts concerning the past. We bring up again in our mind events of the past and we suffer from them. However, they are nothing but thoughts. Moreover they agitate that which does not exist at all: the past is definitively past. Starting from the moment when we understand the present nonexistence of these events, when we understand the lack of significance, use and benefit of these types of thoughts, from then on, they stop harming us.

We have the same attitude toward the future. Thinking of what we should do in the near or distant future creates anxieties and worries and, consequently, suffering. There again, if we think about it carefully, we understand that the future, for the moment, does not exist at all. It is no use to create difficulties for oneself in relationship to that which has no existence.

Meditating on the mind means that one does not follow thoughts which lead toward the future, nor does one follow those that pull one back to the past. One leaves the mind in the present, as it is, without distraction, and without trying to *do* anything.

In this way, a certain experience is born in the mind. Dwelling as long as we can within this experience is meditating. When one meditates like this, one simply remains in the experience without adding anything. One does not say to oneself, "There it is working; there it is not working; here I am; no, I am not here. The mind is empty, in fact, no, it is not empty" and so on. One abides without commentary.

The experience of the meditation implies peace and happiness but remains fundamentally indescribable. It is impossible to say, "This is it" or "This is not it."

KNOWING HOW TO MEDITATE

To learn to meditate correctly, it is not enough to fabricate a personal opinion about what meditation is and to use it as a base. One should receive instructions from a teacher linked with an authentic tradition. It is based on these instructions that one can develop a real experience of meditation.

In particular, nowadays, many people are interested in meditation, but few know how to meditate. Most of them believe that meditating is stopping all thoughts and remaining in that state. This is a mistake. In meditation, one does not try to stop thoughts. One keeps the mind open, relaxed and resting without distraction in the consciousness of the present. In this manner, thoughts can stop by themselves, but one does not do anything to constrain them in order to make them stop.

It sometimes happens that people try to meditate and have some experience of the mind without thoughts, or at least, with very few thoughts. They are happy and say to themselves, "This is it, I am meditating well!" At the other extreme, there are those who get discouraged when so many thoughts appear and feel that they are incapable of meditating. Both attitudes are wrong. If our mind abides a moment without thoughts, we simply remain in this state without thoughts. If it is occupied by thoughts, we abide in the mind with thoughts. One rests in the mind as it is, without passing judgment, "There it is, now it is gone, I am meditating well, I am not meditating well . . . " which would complicate things uselessly.

In meditation, the body should be free of tension, at ease, at rest. One remains silent and breathes naturally. One keeps the mind open, relaxed, without any thoughts of present or future. The mind remains in a state of great openness and relaxation. No voluntary effort is made to do anything, simply to remain present. Under these conditions, meditation becomes very simple.

The meditator will also find it helpful to precede each session with the recitation of a prayer, *mantras*[1] or the offering of a candle. In the *Vajrayana*[2] in particular, the prayer to the spiritual teacher is viewed as a powerful means to develop meditation.

---

[1] *Mantras* are short sacred recitations, the repetition of which helps the mind purify itself and develop its potential for Awakening.

[2] *Vajrayana* or "diamond vehicle" refers to the part of the Buddha's teachings written in texts of an esoteric nature called *tantras*.

Buddha Sakyamuni

Question: What is the significance of meditating for future lives?

Answer: If by meditating, we attain Awakening in this life, we will immensely help other beings through Buddha[1] activity. If this does not happen, the habit of meditation created during this lifetime will allow us to meditate more easily in future lives, and we will progress more quickly.

Question: What is the goal of human life?

Answer: The highest goal that we can attain is to leave samsara[2].

Question: What is karma? What is it that reincarnates?

Answer: It is first necessary to understand how the mind operates. When someone says something pleasant to us, it creates a certain happiness in us. When someone tells us something disagreeable, on the other hand, a certain unhappiness takes shape. That which experiences the pleasant or unpleasant is what we call the mind. If, however, we look at the essence of what is experienced, we find that there is no color, no shape, absolutely nothing material. In this sense, it is said that our mind is empty.

---

[1]When a being attains Awakening, he or she becomes a Buddha. This does not mean that he or she collapses in a kind of insensate state. On the contrary, he or she demonstrates an infinite activity, for the benefit of beings. This activity is spontaneous and impartial but it is not something understandable for us at this point since it is devoid of the notions of subject and object.

[2]*Samsara:* cycle of existence marked by suffering.

Although it is empty, it has the capability of feeling happiness and suffering. It is therefore impossible to say about the mind that it exists, because it is empty, or that it does not exist, because there is feeling.

Let us consider another fact. Suppose that your mind is now occupied with the glass which you find in front of you. Your mind *is* then the thought of the glass. Then you think of another thing in such a way that the previous thought ceases to exist. The passage from a thought to another occurs without any material continuity. There is, however, a continuity within which this process of appearance and cessation of thoughts is situated. This continuity is our mind. We can also understand this continuity of the mind in noticing that in the morning the thought process resumes from the day before, in spite of the interruption of thoughts constituted by deep sleep.

The passage from a past life to a future life unfolds under the same principle. There is a continuity between the mind which experiences the present day and the mind that experiences the following day. The same continuity exists between the mind that experiences the present life, and the mind that experiences the future life. It is the same thing.

Concerning *karma*, it is also necessary to understand that this concerns the mind and that, finally, it is not at all material. *Karma* is in fact like imprints inscribed in our mind and carried by its continuity. Today, for instance, we do something. Then night comes and periods of deep dreamless sleep alternate with periods of dreams where the mind is occupied by other appearances. However, when we wake up tomorrow, we will remember what we did today. This memory is like an imprint on our mind, able to re-actualize itself the day after. The same principle controls *karma*.

This process of karmic imprints is not, however, definitive. We become free of it when we attain Awakening.

Question: Do you think that the technique of mantras is accessible to Westerners?

Answer: External habits and customs are different in the East and in the West. In the spiritual domain, there is no real difference. Perhaps you think that *mantras* are difficult to practice because you do not know exactly what they are. It is instead a lack of information. In reality, the technique of reciting *mantras* is easy for every one.

Question: In Buddhism, is there a concept of God?

Answer: In Buddhism, one considers the notion of God at different levels. At first approach, one conceives of a superior God, creator of heaven, outside oneself, to whom one addresses prayers with faith. A certain realization of the nature of the mind allows us to comprehend, at a deeper level, that the notion of God and heaven are manifestations issuing from our mind. However, the ultimate level of understanding is the realization that God and our own mind are undifferentiated.

Question: You said that the mind was nonmaterial, although the brain is obviously a material substance.

Answer: In the West, one effectively considers that the mind is in the brain. In the East, one considers that it is in the heart. According to the *dharma* the mind is neither in the brain, nor in the heart. In reality, it is nowhere. It tells us also that the physical body is in reality only a production of our mind, in which the brain or the heart serves as support to the functioning of the mind, without being the mind itself nor the creator of the mind.

Question: A teacher seems necessary to guide us on the path of meditation, but one may not always have a teacher at hand.

Answer: It is true that one does not always have a teacher at hand, and it is not necessary. A teacher gives you instructions. Using them as a reference, you meditate for several months or a year. Then, when you have the occasion to meet again with the teacher, you explain to him or her the results or lack of results of your meditation. This will allow the teacher to give you additional instructions.

Concerning the Tibetan tradition, many high lamas come regularly to the West. There are also many "*dharma* centers" at which some lamas reside permanently.

Question: Have many people always meditated in Tibet?

Answer: In Tibet, a very large number of people have always meditated, monks as well as lay people. Material development was very slow and people were not very worried about it. They were above all turned toward a spiritual life.

Question: How do you manage to speak of that which is beyond the mental? And how can any of it remain through translation, as the translator will not have attained the level of realization corresponding to what is said?

Answer: It is true that ultimate reality is beyond words and the intellect. However, the Buddha himself in order to lead beings toward this ultimate reality used many words. They are only indications pointing toward ultimate reality. They do not pretend to express it because it is inexpressible.

These teachings are now recorded in Tibetan and the translator who knows Tibetan, reconveys them accurately in French [or English]. In Tibetan as in French [or English], the words are only a means to indicate that which is beyond the intellect. It would be a contradiction to believe that the words transmit by themselves that which goes beyond them. This is not the case. If you understood neither Tibetan nor French [nor English], your situation would be hopeless. But at least you know French [or English] . . . .

Amitabha

The Three Hindrances

Meditation is recognizing the nature of the mind[1]. This recognition is the most important task that we must accomplish.

For each person, all manners of manifestation are split into two parts: the body which is inner, and phenomena which are outer. But everything is ruled by the mind. It is said that the essence of the body is human, suggesting that the body is not the essence of the mind, rather that the mind is the essence of the body which serves only as prop for it. In a car, the outer elements such as color, shape, size, and so on, are not the essential elements. The essential part of the car is the engine. In the same manner, the "engine" of a human being is the mind. This is why it is so important to know what it really is, and this can be only accomplished through meditation.

---

[1] The term *mind* in Tibetan, has broad implications. It can designate the *psyche* as well as the *being*. However, when one speaks of the "nature of the mind," or "mode of being of the mind," one is referring not to the domain of psychology, but to the *essence* of the mind, beyond all the fluctuations that may affect it.

On this path, we find three major hindrances that we must overcome:

• Attachment to the world, engendered by the belief that phenomena—our body, material goods and so on—are permanent, real and fulfilling;

• Lack of confidence in the *dharma* and in the teachers who transmit the dharma as the only means to access knowledge of the nature of the mind;

• Distraction, through which our mind becomes continually captivated by objects of the senses and does not turn inward.

If we do not overcome these three hindrances, it will not be possible to meditate.

ATTACHMENT TO THE WORLD

To conquer attachment to the world, including to our body and material objects, it is first necessary to rid oneself of the belief that they have a real and independent existence. One must be conscious that, far from being endowed with a permanence founded in their reality, all phenomena change from one instant to another. They are transitory by nature.

Let us first consider our body. From the moment of our conception to the present, each instant, it never ceases to modify itself. From one second to another, it has never been exactly the same. Initially, the embryo developed in the mother's womb, then, after birth, our body progressively changed from infant to child, child to teenager, teenager to adult, following a continual process of modification. The strength of the body is affirmed as it becomes an adult, it stabilizes, then declines as it enters old age. When its vitality becomes totally exhausted, the body will die. This process of aging bounded by birth and death, does not proceed through sudden changes, but by blocks of years, months or days which succeed each other. It is a phenomenon controlled by a process of continual modification, where each instant causes an alteration in regard to the previous instant.

The objects of the external world are subject to the same rules. Let us look at a house. Because we do not perceive the very subtle levels of impermanence, we have the impression that it is the same as it has been for years, the same as it was last month, the same as it was yesterday. If, however, one looks more carefully, one observes that the microscopic molecules of which it is composed have not ceased being modified, and that the house, in reality, ceased to exist in the same form. Even now, from one instant to another, this modification occurs. Since the day it was built, the house has not stopped aging. A day will come when it will be totally useless, will fall to ruins or will be destroyed. It is the succession of alterations which occur each instant that leads it to its demise.

All phenomena of the outer world are subject to the same process. Becoming conscious of their impermanence, as well as that of our body, will reduce the attachment that we have to this life.

In other respects, we are convinced that phenomena are endowed with the capacity to provide us with genuine happiness, whether it be beautiful forms, harmonious sounds, pleasant smells or agreeable tastes. This conviction is one of the roots of our attachment and has no foundation. If one attentively examines happiness provided in this way, one can see that it is not true happiness. By its very nature, it is changing. Even if it first appears as happiness, there is always the threat that it will be transformed into suffering sooner or later.

Long ago, for instance, at the dawn of development of modern science and techniques, people living in the country in the West did not enjoy any comforts in their houses. Given that material progress was first achieved in cities, many people preferred to move, fleeing the difficulties of their living conditions in the country. Electricity, running water, beautiful furniture, and so on were seen as advantages which were bound to bring happiness of the kind that attracted people to move to the city. However, when people became accustomed to these comforts, the sensation of happiness progressively declined, to the point that what once appeared very agreeable, finally appeared boring from time to time. Nowadays, several people residing in cities would prefer to leave and recapture more rustic living conditions, without sophistication, without carpeting, almost without comfort. Furthermore, one sees people who do not appreciate the amenities of modern furniture, and hunt for old, handmade tables and dressers; sometimes these items are rickety and falling apart. The happiness of one moment, because of impermanence, easily becomes the unhappiness of another moment. One can say that a moment of happiness is not really happiness because it is never definitive.

This is why the Buddha compared all pleasure and happiness of this world to honey licked on a sharp blade: one first appreciates the sweetness of the honey but then quickly cuts oneself and feels pain. Without even referring to the words of the Buddha, it is sufficient to look at our own experience: happiness that is transformed into suffering is familiar to us all. If we truly understand this, our attachment to this world, again, will diminish.

Finally, although we accord a self-existence to phenomena of the external world, they are lacking this reality and are only manifestations projected by our own mind. If we refer to a dream, we can understand that phenomena, although lacking self-existence, manifest in our mind external objects, landscapes, houses, and humans. All these appear in a dream. Furthermore, in relationship with these occurrences, we experience agreeable or disagreeable sensations. Everything seems true although it is only the play of our mind. It is said to be the same for the appearances of the world we experience daily. Even if this is difficult for us to experience, we can at least understand how certain qualities that we attribute to the external world are, in fact, colored by our own mind.

For example, when one is under the grasp of great suffering or unhappiness, one will probably perceive the people one meets as ill-disposed toward oneself, or as aggressive. Let us imagine that we are very unhappy or angry. Even if one serves us a good meal in an agreeable place, it will not seem good to us. If on the other hand, we are happy, for one reason or another, even a mediocre meal served in insignificant surroundings will seem delicious. It is not the meal itself that is good or bad, it is our mind that imposes the quality. Therefore, one can understand at least partially how external phenomena depend on our mind.

Understanding that everything is impermanent, that happiness is transformed into suffering, and that all phenomena are lacking reality in themselves and are only projections of our mind, will permit us to counteract the first hindrance to meditation, that is, our attachment to this world.

LACK OF TRUST

The second hindrance to meditation is the lack of trust in the *dharma* and in the teacher. For confidence to develop we must first receive information, listen to the teachings given by teachers, then reflect on and examine this information. To the extent that what we have heard appears worthy of our interest, an initial level of trust will take shape in our mind.

Let us clarify this with an example. A person who is very sick, would want proper treatment to cure him or herself. He or she would first listen to the advice of other people and would choose to see a physician based on their recommendations. He or she could not be certain of the value of the physician and treatment, but would simply be predisposed to have a favorable opinion. This is the beginning of trust. "Since everyone has spoken highly of the physician and treatment, it is here that I feel I would have the best chance of being cured."

The physician would then examine the sick person, and prescribe a treatment to follow over a certain amount of time. If, after having followed this treatment for several days, the patient begins to see an improvement, to gain back his or her strength and have less pain, he or she would not only have a favorable opinion, but his or her trust would be affirmed. Finally, if the person is completely cured, trust in the value of the treatment and in the capabilities of the physician would be completely confirmed, and certainty would develop.

All beings in *samsara* are similar to sick people, the *dharma* is comparable to the treatment, and the master who teaches the *dharma* to the physician. In the same way it is necessary to take the medicine for a certain amount of time to determine its value, it is also necessary to try practicing the *dharma* and meditation to get an idea of what it can bring us. Simply hearing or receiving information, even if it is necessary, is not sufficient. It would be like receiving a treatment but not applying it.

Practicing the *dharma* is certain to benefit us, but the effect is always gradual. Some people expect to make progress extremely quickly. They think that they will obtain Awakening, pull up the roots of suffering and taste an abundance of happiness in a very short time. The facts will soon refute this and, not having obtained the hoped-for result, they risk saying to themselves, "I do not see much progress—this method must not be very good." Obviously, great progress cannot happen so quickly. However, the practice of the *dharma* does lead to visible changes known by those who are effectively engaged on the path.

By seeking and receiving information, above all by practice, confidence and trust are born. These overcome the second hindrance.

DISTRACTION

Our mind is constantly distracted by external objects. This is the third hindrance to meditation.

The distractions that disturb our mind may be related to the past, present or future, but in fact it is the past and future that occupy us most of the time, and consequently create the most suffering.

The past can be yesterday, last month, last year or further away in time. Often, the past that preoccupies us is that which was not well-lived, that in which we were unsuccessful, where bad experiences happened to us and where we made mistakes. We come back to this painful past and we suffer again uselessly. Let us take an example of a mistake. Whether it occurred yesterday, last month or last year, it is now done and nothing can undo it or prevent it from having been done. But it is now finished. Bringing up this mistake in mind, thinking about it incessantly and suffering over it, merely creates useless suffering in ourselves. The mistake or the situation in which we found ourselves is past and no longer exists. If by thinking about it again and again, we could erase the mistake, prevent it from having been made, or cause the event not to have happened, it would be useful to turn back the clock. But this is not the case; we cannot undo the past. Let us leave it alone! With our thoughts, we create useless suffering such as this about events that no longer exist.

Even more numerous than thoughts concerning the past, and creating even more suffering, are the thoughts about the future. We might find ourselves somewhere where we have everything we need at our disposal and where there is nothing to cause us present suffering. In this apparently happy situation, we may, however, begin to worry about all kinds of future problems: "Will I always have the same comforts, will I encounter difficulties in my job, will I be able to keep it," and so on. In this manner, we do not enjoy the peace of the present moment, rather we substitute it for suffering about a situation that does not exist. Most of our suffering comes from the future as we envision it. Our illusory thoughts are really strange phenomena! The future, for the moment, is not here at all, but we turn toward it in order to suffer. Moreover, although the future contingencies offer two aspects—favorable and unfavorable—we almost always choose the second one. Seeing things in a favorable aspect would be like thinking, "Concerning my job, my house, my work, and so on, I believe everything will go well, things will be fine." But this is rarely the way we envision it. Rather we tend to think, "I will not succeed. This will not work. I do not believe that this will be possible." Thus, most of our suffering comes from considering the future.

If we look at the present, without turning toward the past or future, in general, we simply do not have any suffering.

While meditating, one should never give free reign to thoughts of the past or future. Meditating, in fact, will not present any difficulty if one has properly understood the method. We do not follow thoughts that concern the past or future. We maintain a relaxed mind, just as it is in the present moment. It is then very easy! When we leave the mind relaxed in the present, there is no suffering. Meditation should always be like this; not following thoughts of the past or future, the mind rests in the present, relaxed and non-grasping.

When one meditates like this, one rests for moments

without thoughts; but our mind does not always remain in this state and then thoughts arise again.

Many people believe meditation must necessarily be a state devoid of all thoughts; or if while they meditate thoughts appear, they conclude that they are incapable of meditating, that meditating is an exercise completely beyond their reach. This, *a priori*, is a mistake: meditating is not eliminating thoughts.

How should one approach this problem of thoughts? First, it is important to avoid two mistakes:
• The first is to be conscious that thoughts produce themselves and then to follow them mechanically;
• The second is to try to stop them.

The correct view is, on the contrary, to be conscious of the production of thoughts but neither to follow them nor to try to stop them and simply not to worry about them. If one is not preoccupied with thoughts, they do not have any strength. As long as one does not know the nature of one's mind, the latter produces thoughts which may be positive as well as negative, endowed with great power over us, because we grasp them as real. In the absence of this grasping, thoughts have no strength.

When one leaves one's mind relaxed, a moment will come when one rests without thoughts. This stable state is like an ocean without waves. Within this stability a thought arises. This thought is like a wave which forms on the surface of the ocean. To the extent that one leaves this thought alone without doing anything about it, without "seizing" it, it vanishes by itself in the mind where it came from. It is like the wave that vanishes again into the sea from where it arose.

The ocean and the wave, if one does not reflect upon them, could appear as two separate realities. In fact, they are undifferentiated in essence, because the essence of the wave is water, just as the essence of the ocean is also water. One cannot say that they are two different entities.

Waves arise on the surface of the ocean, but they cannot do anything else but blend again into the ocean. One cannot say that the ocean will decrease in the first instance or that it will increase in the second. In the same manner, when one leaves the movement of thoughts without interfering with them, our mind does not deteriorate when thoughts are produced, nor is it improved without them.

As long as we do not understand the mind, we are a little like a person at the seashore who wants to rid the ocean of waves. When a wave comes toward him or her, he or she wants to take it and throw it to one side, and then take the following one and throw it to the other side. Even if, independent of his or her efforts, the ocean is calm for a few moments, it is inevitable that the waves will form again. The person who hopes to establish an ocean forever free of waves will constantly be disappointed. Wanting to eliminate thoughts during meditation is placing oneself in the same situation.

Even though waves arise out of the ocean, they return to it. In reality, the ocean and the waves are not different. Understanding this, we can take a seat on the beach and relax without fatigue or difficulty. Similarly, when we look at the essence of our mind, whether or not there are thoughts is not important: we remain simply relaxed.

This is the way to overcome the third hindrance, distraction: by keeping the mind relaxed in the present.

These three points that we have just considered are extremely important. The essentials of meditation are included in them.

Question: What becomes of meditation when one falls under the grasp of sleepiness or laziness?

Answer: To resolve the problem of sleepiness, there are several remedies. First, one must recognize that this sleepiness is the effect of karmic veils. In order to dissipate them, it is good to offer candles in front of a representation of the Buddha. This light, because of the interdependence of phenomena, will help us to free ourselves from sleepiness. At the same time, it is very important to develop devotion for one's spiritual teacher. Finally, during meditation, one should keep one's mind slightly alert, keep oneself very straight, wear clean clothes and, if possible, place oneself in a well-ventilated place.

Question: We are always projecting ourselves into the future. When one is a child, one studies with the view of becoming an adult. Throughout one's life, one is motivated by that which one wishes to accomplish later. What would therefore constitute spontaneous action in the present that would not involve projection toward the future?

Answer: In order not to be seized by thoughts attached to the future, one should see that all phenomena are impermanent, illusory, and distressing as we discussed earlier. As long as we consider the world to be real, the future seems very important to us. It seems indispensable for us to think about the future. If, on the contrary, one reflects upon impermanence, upon the distressing nature of all phenomena and their illusory character, one assigns them less importance. This will automatically lessen our preoccupation with the future. What is essential, then, is to maintain the mind without distraction in the consciousness of the present.

If one is entirely involved in the practice of the *dharma*, one can totally abandon worries about the future. However, even if one maintains certain ordinary activities that require one to be preoccupied with the future, through the practice of the *dharma*, this obsession with the future will decrease. One who knows the nature of the mind well, who possesses great realization, can make as many plans for the future as he or she wishes. He or she has in effect the knowledge that these plans, as well as the one who conceives them, are phenomena lacking self-existence, that they are similar to magical creations, simple appearances without reality, and he or she acts within the context of this knowledge. This person may from then on look like an ordinary being, but there is in truth a great difference from the point of view of the experience or non-experience of suffering. We beginners attribute great reality to our thoughts of the future. This is why they are causes of suffering. It is not the same for a realized being.

Suppose, for example, that you are doing office work and that you have some very important letters to write. On your way to work, and once you arrive, you will turn over and over in your head the problem of these letters, "If I write them this way, am I expressing myself in the best way? Or perhaps, it would be better to say it this way... Unless of course it would be taken like this . . . . " You think continually about what you have to do. Furthermore, it is possible that you view your projects pessimistically and imagine more causes of failure than possibilities of success. You are uneasy, worried, and in other words, you suffer.

It is true that we cannot now, all at once, give up all of our preoccupations about the future. It is possible that these preoccupations will create a certain amount of suffering for us. But at least from time to time, we can decide not to turn toward the future, and although it will be for only a few minutes, we can maintain the mind at rest in the consciousness of the present. Furthermore, and this is very important, when we look at the future, we should learn to be positive. Always seeing the negative side of things will only help to increase our inner difficulties. It is a little like a watch with a winding mechanism: if we wind it too tightly, we will end up breaking the mechanism. Through worrying about the future, tensions become greater and greater and there is a risk of breakdown.

Question: Is it necessary to have a lama to practice the dharma? How should one look for a qualified teacher?

Answer: One meets a teacher by the strength of one's *karma* and through one's aspiration. If one has a profound wish, one will naturally find a teacher.

Chenrezig

PRACTICING MEDITATION

Mental Calming– "Shinay"

The Four Reflections

In order to realize in this life through the practice of *mahamudra*[1], the ultimate non-death as the true mode of being of the mind, one must first be conscious of:

• the transitory nature of all manifested phenomena,

• the difficulty of obtaining a human existence among all the possibilities of rebirth,

• the inevitability of the effects of our acts which predetermine the happy or painful nature of our future lives,

• and the inherence of suffering in all types of conditioned existence.

Unless one reflects upon these four points intently and completely saturates oneself with them, deep

---

[1]The term *mahamudra* (*the great seal*) designates the revelation of the ultimate nature of the mind, free of all illusion and error. It is customary to designate three levels:

- ultimate mind, which is in a potential state in every being;

- the path that leads to the actualization of this potential including mental pacification and superior vision;

- actualization itself, as meditation and as a permanent state.

meditation is impossible.

The Four Specific Preliminaries[1]

The next step is to fix one's attention and increase one's confidence through the practice of *taking Refuge*. This is the foundation of the path of Buddha. Along with Refuge the right motivation is necessary for development of the *bodhicitta*, or the *mind of awakening*. Bodhicitta is the aspiration to attain awakening, not for oneself, but in order to become capable of helping all beings.

Second, one must purify oneself of the obscurations and impurities one has accumulated since time without beginning. This purification is accomplished through the practice of *Dorje Sempa* (Sanskrit, *Vajrasattva*).

One must not only try to free oneself of mental obstacles but positively restructure the mind through accumulation of merit and accumulation of wisdom. This is accomplished through the *offering of the mandala*.

Finally, one opens one's mind to the grace of the spiritual teacher by the practice of *spiritual union* (Sanskrit, *Guru Yoga*).

These four specific preliminary practices must be done with diligence.

The Four Conditions

Causal Condition: All of the aspects of the cycle of conditioned existence (Sanskrit, *samsara*) are by their very nature suffering. This is not to say that happiness is totally absent, but it is passing, superficial, unauthentic, and fundamentally changing. Recognizing the painful nature of the cycle of existence and aspiring to the realization of the ultimate mode of being of the mind, the *mahamudra*, which liberates one, is the causal condition [i.e., motivation] of meditation, the initial impetus to enter the path.

---

[1]The specific preliminaries mentioned here properly belong to the *Vajrayana* context, in other words the *tantras*. The explanation of their practice should be received from a qualified lama.

However, as long as we consider our situation in the world as happy, we will have no reason to divert ourselves from it.

Main Condition: The aspiration to liberate oneself is not sufficient in itself. It is indispensable that the path be shown by a teacher. Upon the causal condition the main condition should be grafted. The teacher can be described as four aspects, the first one is required in order to access the other three:

The human person as a teacher: the one who exposes the spiritual path to us and shows us the mode of being of the mind. Being content with reading books is not sufficient as a first approach. Only the spoken words of a teacher can impress a sufficiently deep conviction within us.

The word of the Buddha as a teacher: once the different facets of the *dharma* are understood, and once the comprehension of the mode of being of the mind is acquired through the explanations of a teacher, having begun to meditate, we can confront our experience with the perfect word of the Buddha as well as with the commentaries and treatises written by competent masters. We will then be able to examine the validity and meaning of our inner discoveries.

Appearances as a teacher: when we have acquired a sufficient experience through meditation as well as a system of theoretical references upon which we may rely, external appearances become the supports of meditation. As the earth is the solid foundation upon which humans and animals live, plants grow, and buildings are erected, wherein rests every possibility of existence in our world, so faith and trust are the fundamental firmament upon which a spiritual path is possible. Therefore, seeing the earth will be a reminder of faith. A continuous flow of water in a river is an example of what our effort should be: a continuous perseverance. Fire symbolizes the fire of wisdom. The movement of the wind reminds us of the transitory and changing nature of phenomena. When thus perceived, appearances evoke a correspondence with the elements of our inner path, and they therefore function as a spiritual teacher[1].

The ultimate reality as teacher: finally we will develop the realization that all phenomena, outer or inner, animate or inanimate, do not exist in a separate mode, but are the expression of the clarity of the mind itself. This realization of the indivisibility of outer appearances and mind means that the ultimate reality has become the spiritual teacher.

The Objective Condition: this defines the right object of meditation, in other words, meditating knowingly: the mind of the meditator remains free of mental superimposition, one's experience is devoid of commentaries such as "my mind is clear," or "my mind is happy," or "my mind is empty." The mind is left free, as it is naturally. Meditation does not add anything to the naturally simple space-like and peaceful state of the mind. One does not meditate *on* something in the way one would fabricate a new state to add to what the mind already is in itself. Meditation is rediscovery of the mind's natural state. The mind dwells without distraction in its own essence, in

---

[1]During a teaching, Bokar Rinpoche gave the people of Nice an example that illustrates how appearances can serve as a teacher.

"The people of Nice entertain a privileged relationship with the sea: some people make a living from it, others like to bathe in it, go boating or indulge in other water activities, while others simply enjoy contemplating it. In one way or another, the sea is part of the life and landscape of everyone. Well, each time you see the sea or think about the sea, may it be for you the symbol of love and compassion."

"In Nice, everyone also likes the sun to shine and provide warmth on the beach or they may simply appreciate the luminosity it spreads. Every time you see the sun, think about the sun, may it be for you the symbol and reminder of wisdom."

"In this way, compassion and wisdom will become more and more present in your mind."

its own mode of being. Understanding meditation in this way is the objective condition.

The Immediate Condition: "To leave the mind as it is, without mental intervention, is this really meditating?" "I hope that my meditation will be good." "May my meditation not be bad!" Such doubts, hopes and fears contradict the mind of meditation. One simply dwells in the present. To eliminate hopes and fears is the immediate condition.

* * *

We have considered in total twelve elements, divided in three groups:

The four fundamental reflections, also called the four common preliminaries:
- the transitory nature of phenomena
- the rarity of human existence
- the inevitability of consequences of acts
- the suffering as characteristic of conditioned existence

The four specific preliminaries:
- *taking Refuge* and developing *bodhicitta*
- purification through the practice of *Dorje Sempa*[1]
- accumulation of merit through *mandala offering*
- the opening to grace through spiritual union.

The four conditions:
- the causal condition
- the main condition
- the objective condition
- the immediate condition.

---

[1]*Dorje Sempa* is a deity of the *Vajrayana* that is the vehicle for the force of the purification of Awakening. The practice includes a visualization as well as recitation of a *mantra*. It acts at the level of unconscious conditioning, neutralizing existing negative effects.

Dorje Sempa

The gathering of these twelve elements creates the ideal context for meditation.

Some people tend to think that only meditation is important, that the preliminary practices are superfluous and that the conditions are only auxiliary. In a hurry to meditate, they view the rest as a hindrance. However, beginning without preparation will not lead to effective meditation. To grow a flower requires not only a seed but also a human hand and a tool to work the soil; then the seed must receive some water, warmth and fertilizer. Without these additional elements, the seed, although primordial in the process, will never produce a flower. To approach the meditation of *mahamudra*, which leads to the recognition of the ultimate nature of the mind and, as a result, to its liberation, it is also necessary to gather the twelve elements mentioned above.

THE BODY IN PRACTICE

BODILY POSTURE

The complete posture includes seven points:
• crossed legs in the *adamantine posture*, the left foot resting on the right thigh and the right foot on the left thigh,
• spine straight like an arrow,
• shoulders are open like the wings of a vulture[1],
• hands in the meditation *mudra*[2], right hand resting on the left hand, palms upward,

---

[1]Vultures are considered as very helpful and good in Tibetan culture contrarily to what they evoke in some Western traditions.

[2]*Mudra* designates a symbolic posture of the hands, static or dynamic.

• chin forming a right angle with the throat,
• eyes gazing in space, slanting downward, in the direction of an imaginary point situated four to eight fingers in front of your nose,
• mouth and tongue are relaxed.

Far from being arbitrary, each point of the posture has its justification in relation with the system of subtle energies traversing our body, tightly linked to the production of thoughts[1].

PLACING THE MIND

With the body established in the correct posture, one must then avoid mental tension which results from the fixation on the idea "I am meditating." The mind remains relaxed, open, space-like and clear, neither getting lost in

---

[1]A slightly simplified posture exists and is comprised of five points. It is the same as the seven point posture excluding the positions of the shoulders and mouth.

Crossing the legs in the *adamantine posture* is often difficult for most Westerners; in this case, one can rest in the *bodhisattva posture*: the left heel is wedged against the perineum, the right foot and leg are bent flat in front. Unless one is naturally flexible or particularly accustomed to the posture, it is generally necessary to raise the buttocks with a hard, rather thick cushion.

The relationship between posture, circulation of winds in the subtle channels and consequent perturbations of the mind is well illustrated by the mental distortions caused by an incorrect position of the trunk, and therefore the vertebra and axis of the body:
- If one leans slightly toward the left, it is traditionally explained that one will fall first into a sense of well-being, which will degenerate into desire.
- If one leans forward, one senses an absence of thoughts, which will degenerate into mental obscurity.
- If one leans backward, one has a sensation of vacuity, which will degenerate into a feeling pride.
- If one leans toward the right, one has a feeling of clarity, which will degenerate into a feeling of pride.

remembering the past nor in thinking of the future, nor mistaking the reality of the thoughts of the present. It remains in a state of vigilance, without distraction, open to itself as it is without tension. The meditator should not have the sensation of being in a deep, dark gorge, clouded with fog but rather on the summit of a mountain, where the altitude and limpidity of the sky permit one to clearly see the entire horizon. The correct manner of placing the mind is essential. There is often a tendency to approach meditation in a very tense manner, in a state of forced non-distraction. Without knowing how to first relax one's mind, leaving it open and content, it is not possible to meditate. This is a necessary condition.

(meditation)[1]

MEDITATION EXERCISES

The mind resting like this, one applies oneself with concentration on the chosen object, initially in the context of mental calming (Tibetan, *shinay*). Many methods are possible. We will further explore some of them here. *Shinay* can first be practiced using a pure or impure[2] support.

---

[1]The word meditation in parentheses indicates moments of silence during which meditation was practiced when these teachings were given.

[2]The terms *pure* and *impure* do not refer here to some arbitrary ritual observances but to the essential nature of the object of meditation. The ordinary appearances we perceive are said to be impure because they are the fruit of our karmic conditioning and subsequently of the functioning of a mind polluted by different veils hindering it: ignorance, dualistic grasping, conflicting emotions and *karma*. On the other hand, all objects have a sacred character originating from the total purity of the Awakened Mind. Each object is in essence the expression of grace and compassion. Impure and pure, in fact, describe less the object in itself than its origin. It is obvious that for an Awakened Being the distinction does not apply.

The notion of an impure support refers to any object of an ordinary nature that one selects as a focus of concentration: a mountain, hill, building, table, glass or any other object. One puts one's mind in a relaxed state and without distraction.

We could for instance meditate on the seat in front of us. Concentration in this context does not imply indulgence in a discursive examination of the characteristics of the object: its form, height, surface, upholstery, nature and nuances of the cloth, and so on. Neither is it a matter of projecting one's mind as if to place it inside the seat. With ourselves in one place and the seat in another, it is simply placing our mind on what it sees, without distraction, without being carried away by other thoughts, and without tension.

(meditation)

Some of you succeeded no doubt in stabilizing your mind in a satisfactory manner on the object of concentration; others will have been present for a few moments, but sometimes lost in other thoughts. This alternation can happen very quickly. Whatever the circumstances, one should not force the concentration but work with the conditions as they occur, relaxed and open to the situation.

Second, a pure support designates any representation, symbolic or not, which has a sacred character.

We can, for instance, visualize the body of the Buddha in the space in front of us, mentally creating a clear, luminous, radiant and perfectly proportioned image on which we concentrate without distraction.

(meditation)

Dorje Sempa

It is likely that this image will have appeared, sometimes clearly, sometimes in a confused fleeting manner in our mind, and sometimes it will have been totally absent. This is not so important. Trying to meditate like this is good in and of itself, and regular repetition of the exercise will lead to a clearer and more stable visualization. The alternation between clarity and confusion—even the inability to visualize—is a normal phenomenon for beginners. Perseverance will progressively refine your capabilities.

Another example of the use of a pure support is to imagine a small sphere of very bright and very intense, white light (Tibetan, *tigle*; Sanskrit, *bindu*) at the level of your forehead. This support is pure because one considers it symbolically undifferentiated from the spiritual teacher.

(*meditation*)

Finally, *shinay* can be practiced without a support. The mind is left free, relaxed, and at the same time in a state of non-distraction.

(*meditation*)

Thus we have seen four possibilities for concentration:
• on an impure support
• on a pure support:
  . either the body of the Buddha
  . or a small sphere of light.
• without a support.

Some people will have discovered, no doubt, a more particular affinity for the first type of exercise, some with the second, some with the third, and some with the fourth. Other individuals will not have any marked preference. In the first case, the best is to proceed with daily practice using the method of your choice. In the second case, you can practice each method alternatively. Whatever you choose, only regular practice and perseverance will facilitate your progress on the path of mental calming.

DEALING WITH THOUGHTS

Beginners, not being very familiar with the meditation, often expect to experience a perfectly calm mind totally free of thoughts. They fear the coming of thoughts and when thoughts arise they are upset by the inability to meditate. Fearing thoughts, being irritated or disturbed by their appearance, or believing that the absence of thoughts is a good thing in itself, are errors which will lead to useless frustration and feelings of guilt.

The mind of a person who does not meditate, a beginner or an experienced meditator is traversed by thoughts, but the manner in which they deal with them, varies considerably from one to another.

Someone not practicing meditation is, in relation to his or her thoughts, similar to a blind person facing a distant highway. The blind person is unable to see whether cars are passing or not. Similarly, an ordinary person, while feeling a vague sense of discomfort and inner uneasiness, is not conscious of the flow of thoughts which nevertheless continue without interruption.

Beginning to meditate, one discovers that one can see but one would like there to be no cars passing. If just one car passes, our expectations are destroyed. A second is a further disappointment. With a third one, we become irritated and so on. The naive hope of an empty highway is forever dashed. One is at the same time conscious and unhappy about the succession of vehicles. Each car that passes is seen as a new difficulty. One revolts against an inevitable state of things. In the same manner, when one sees meditation as a space devoid of thoughts, each thought that comes obviously contradicts the preconceived scenario; one is in a situation of almost permanent failure.

When, on the other hand, one has better understood what meditation really is, one observes cars passing, but without rejecting or revolting against them, and without having decided that the highway should be empty. One should not expect the absence of cars, neither should one fear their presence. The cars pass and one lets them pass. They are neither harmful nor beneficial. If thoughts arise in meditation, one lets them naturally pass, without being attached to them or condemning them; if they do not arise, one does not find particular satisfaction in this. A sane approach to thoughts is the condition of a good meditation.

People with a misconception of meditation believe that all thoughts should cease. We cannot, in fact, establish ourselves in a state devoid of thoughts. The fruit of meditation is not the absence of thoughts, but the fact that thoughts cease to harm us. Once enemies, they become friends.

A bad meditation generally comes from negligence of preliminary practices; even if these have been completed, it can also come from a misunderstanding of the correct way to place the mind.

Ordinary people are perpetually in a state of mental distraction, their minds scattered. When one meditates, on the other hand, the greatest obstacles come from additional mental productions, from the commentaries one makes on oneself, and one's preconceptions. Genuine meditation is avoidance of distraction as well as of any additional mental activity.

Further Information on Mental Calming– "Shinay"

Meditation leads to the discovery of the mind. What is our mind? We have only a superficial idea of what it is. For us, it is that part of us that feels happiness and suffering, and is conscious of our field of experience. Except for this, we do not know what it really is.

All beings have always[1] existed along with their mind. At no moment are they separated from it. However, they do not know what it truly is, its essence.

It is because of this lack of knowledge of the truth of what our mind is that we endure suffering, difficulties, and the confrontation with that which we do not wish, everything that makes up *samsara*.

---

[1]Buddhism does not consider that beings are the creation of a superior God who places them in time, but rather considers them as having existed since time without beginning.

Because it will be the end of our suffering, this knowledge is indispensable to us. However, there are no worldly means which will give us access to it. Only the spiritual path, the *dharma*, allows us to discover what we truly are.

In particular, within the *Vajrayana*, the recognition of the ultimate nature of the mind is made possible by the grace of the teacher, called a *lama*[1]. A *lama* in this case is meant in the full sense of the word: a person who is endowed with a deep realization. What is this grace? Non-material and invisible, it is like a force or an extremely strong current under the influence of which we place ourselves through our trust and devotion.

In the *Kagyupa* lineage, one of the four great schools of Tibetan Buddhism with which we are affiliated, this transmission of grace originated with the primordial Buddha Vajradhara[2]. It was received, first by the great Indian yogi Tilopa who conferred it to his disciple Naropa. It was passed then to Tibet through Marpa and continued there with Milarepa, Gampopa, and the first Karmapa. Finally it has arrived in our time through the succession of Karmapas. It is a lineage of uninterrupted transmission that is called the "Golden Rosary."

In order to open ourselves to this grace, we can pray to the Karmapa or any other *lama* that we regard as our teacher by considering that he or she is seated on a lotus above our head. At the end of the prayer, we

---

[1]*Lama* designates a person with a deep accomplishment who acts toward all the beings with a great compassion.

[2]Vajradhara, in Tibetan *Dorje Chang*, is considered to be the form taken by the Buddha to reveal the *Vajrayana* to beings with particular faculties.

conceive that the *lama* melts into light, and that this light is absorbed into us. In this way, we receive the grace fully, our body, speech and mind having become one with the Body, Speech and Mind of the teacher.

MEASURING OUR GOOD FORTUNE

The diversity of beings is great. If we simply consider animals which we can observe easily, we see how the condition of their existence is difficult and painful. If we had to endure the same suffering as they do, we would understand even better their situation. By comparison we are very fortunate to have a human existence.

If we look at humans themselves, we notice that a lot of them are taken up with negative activities and that, through these activities, they accumulate the causes of much future suffering. On the other hand, on our side, we have the great fortune to know the *dharma*, to find qualified teachers and to have the possibility of studying and practicing a spiritual path. If we do not reflect carefully, we will probably not understand at this point how fortunate we are. Often, it is only when we are touched by unhappiness that we are conscious of the value of our previous happiness. When we are healthy, we do not necessarily appreciate the value of this state. But when we become ill and have to go to the hospital, lose our freedom of movement and endure painful treatments, we then understand the value of the health we have lost. In a similar way, we must become conscious of the favorable situation in which we find ourselves now. In particular, because of the *dharma*, because of meditation, we have the opportunity to progress toward recognition of the ultimate nature of our mind, which is also the end of all suffering.

Meditation includes two stages:
- mental calming, in Tibetan *shinay*;
- superior vision, in Tibetan *lhatong*.

One can also consider the union of *shinay* and *lhatong* to constitute a third stage.

These three levels, however, do not exist from the point of view of the ultimate nature of the mind itself, but simply as a description of the path.

POSTURE

First one must adopt a physical posture that favors meditation. Movement of the body provokes an agitation of the subtle winds[1] that itself engenders agitation of the mind. The Tibetan term *shinay* is composed as follows: *shi* means "to calm" and *nay* "to dwell." Therefore it means that one "calms" the body, speech, and mind and that one "dwells" in this peaceful state.

The posture is important because it allows the energy channels to be aligned. When they are not straight, the subtle winds cannot circulate well which creates mental agitation.

The complete posture consists of seven points:

1- The legs are crossed in the *vajra* position, which is similar to the lotus position, but instead one places first the left foot on the right thigh and then the right foot on the left thigh. If one cannot adopt this position, one can take another called the *bodhisattva* posture, with the left foot against the perineum, and the right foot placed flat in front of the left.

---

[1] See note page 6.

2- One places the hands in the *mudra*[1] of the meditation, the right hand resting on the left hand
3- One keeps the back very straight.
4- The shoulders are relaxed but slightly pulled back.
5- One draws in the chin slightly.
6- The tongue and mouth are relaxed.
7- One gazes into space, eyes angling downward and fixed on a virtual point that is about eight fingers placed laterally in front of the tip of the nose.

This seven-point posture mentioned earlier is considered to be the most favorable posture for the optimal circulation of the winds. It is called *Vairocana's* posture.

THREE SUPPORTS FOR THE MIND

Once the body is stabilized, we must learn to stabilize the mind. In the first place, we should not follow thoughts concerning the past, nor should we follow those on the future, but remain relaxed and quiet with the mind in the present. At the same time, we may rely on a support. We will look at three of them:

Breathing

We direct our attention to the natural movement of our breathing, considering that our breathing and the mind are one. We follow inhaling and exhaling with the mind relaxed and without distraction.

A white *tigle*

We imagine that, at the base of our forehead, is a small sphere of light or white *tigle* producing brilliant light. As before, we keep the mind focused on the *tigle*, while considering that the *tigle* and the mind are one.

---

[1]*Mudra*: see page 65.

The Buddha

Undifferentiated from our mind, the Buddha *Sakyamuni* is found in our heart, the size of our thumb, clear and brilliant. We focus our attention on this visualization.

In this type of meditation, we compare our mind to a wild elephant, our attention to the rope that attaches it, and the support on which we concentrate to the trunk of the tree to which the rope is tied.

SHINAY WITHOUT A SUPPORT

In *shinay* without a support, the mind remains concentrated on itself, on the letting go and on not acting. There is no object on which the mind is directed, but we rest vigilant and without distraction. Some thoughts may come, but we do not attempt to stop them, nor follow them.

In order to illustrate this type of meditation, we can use the comparison of a pole and flag. When the wind is not blowing, neither the pole nor the flag move. When the wind blows the flag moves but the pole does not. Thoughts are similar to the flag. The mind, conscious and vigilant, is similar to the pole that does not move, whether there are thoughts or not. Without following nor attempting to stop the thoughts, one keeps the mind both relaxed and non-distracted.

SLEEPINESS AND AGITATION

Practicing *shinay* one meets two main obstacles: sleepiness and agitation. They are the two enemies of *shinay*. Everyone meets them depending on one's nature.

For some, sleepiness will dominate, for others, it is agitation that takes over. Everyone must see which difficulty affects him or her the most, and apply the corresponding remedy.

When one has a tendency toward sleepiness, one needs to tense one's mind, to open one's eyes widely and to think that one is looking at the sky.

When, at the other extreme, one is seized by agitation, carried away by many thoughts, one should relax, close one's eyes and imagine that one is looking toward the ground.

It is important to be conscious of these difficulties in our meditation and to know how to correctly remedy them, otherwise we risk increasing them. The person who is inclined to sleepiness, whose mind seems dull and obscure, and who, while meditating, tries to achieve a state of excessive relaxation, will attain only a profound sleepiness. This is not a meditation but mental dullness. At the opposite extreme, the one who is agitated by numerous thoughts and who approaches meditation in a tense manner thinking obstinately, "I *am* going to meditate," will only increase the production of thoughts, will not feel at ease, and in fact, will not be able to meditate either. This is why it is very necessary to diagnose one's problem precisely.

It seems that in Tibet and in the East in general, the tendency toward sleepiness dominates, while in the West agitation is the main problem. Whichever it is, when one practices *shinay*, it is important to place one's body, speech and mind in a state of ease and openness. The mind should feel happy, without fidgeting. One should not feel a sensation of being in a narrow, closed room, but rather to have the feeling of being outdoors, in a pleasant place. It is indispensable to be at ease, relaxed and open. These are the cornerstones of meditation.

FROM THE RIVER TO THE OCEAN

The mind should not be distracted by thoughts of past or future. It rests in the present, just as it is in itself, without distraction.

The Indian yogi Tilopa said, "The mind tied up with tensions will unravel without any doubt if it relaxes." From time without beginning, we are bound by thoughts which result in great tension. In meditation, this is undone and one rests at ease. The consciousness of the present, the mind resting in its own nature, should be devoid of any tension.

When we meditate in this way, it is possible that we will experience a short period without thoughts. However, soon thoughts will arise. As beginners, we perhaps believe that we should not have any thoughts. This is a mistake; it is enough to remain vigilant and non-distracted.

Gampopa, the principal disciple of Milarepa said, "All meditators value the state without thoughts, but not being able to close the door to thoughts, they tire themselves with the effort."

Generally, the mind of beginners is busy with many thoughts. One traditionally compares this state to a stream going down a steep mountainside. One can then tell oneself, "I have so many thoughts that it is useless for me to continue. I will never be able to do it! It would be better to quit. Ah, yes! If I did not have any thoughts, I could say that I meditate, but in my case, it is no use." On the contrary, one should not quit meditating, it is natural for beginners to meet this stream of thoughts.

In persevering, one acquires a certain habit of meditation and, with experience, thoughts become a river which slowly flows into the plains. Finally, the mind is able to rest without thoughts, becoming an ocean without waves.

One must understand that it is a progression, that

one state will succeed to another only after a long and regular practice of meditating. The beginner must not believe that he or she should, from the first session on, be able to access the state where thoughts are absent. This would be impossible for the beginner.

It is not useful to think, "I absolutely must not have any thoughts while meditating—no thought should enter my mind!" One should simply maintain a mental attitude in which one considers that if some thoughts arise, it is of no importance; if there are no thoughts, it is also not important. What is important is remaining non-distracted.

CLARITY AND ABSENCE OF THOUGHTS

When the mind calms down naturally and remains thought-free, this is *shinay*. Nevertheless, there is correct and incorrect *shinay*.

The incorrect *shinay* is to be without thoughts, but at the same time to find oneself in a kind of obscurity. In fact, one is closer to sleep than *shinay*. Some people who have not understood meditation, establish themselves in an indefinite state where they think of nothing and tell themselves, "Oh, how well I meditate, how content I am!" In reality they are not meditating at all.

The positive *shinay*, on one hand, shares with deep sleep an absence of thoughts, but it differs by the disappearance of the obscurity. The clarity of mind has taken its place. The absence of thoughts combined with clarity is the true *shinay*. It is an experience that can only come naturally and progressively. Some people may experience it quickly, but in general, this is not the case. The difference between clarity and non-clarity is not conceptual. It is not sufficient to think, "Well, from now on I am going to establish myself in clarity. I am going to keep my mind clear." It is not a state that can be created by mental faculties. It is a component of the nature of the mind itself.

Suppose that at night, with the light off, you have a glass of water in front of you. You can distinguish the object clearly. You suppose that it is a glass, but you are unable to recognize what it contains. There is a dark liquid, but you cannot see if it is water or something else. This is *shinay* without clarity. On the contrary, during the day you have no difficulty seeing the glass, identifying its contents, and perceiving all the details. This clear vision is similar to the clarity of *shinay*.

It is important to understand this distinction between true and false *shinay* in order to be able to recognize, in the future, whether one is on the wrong road or not. This does not mean that you should think you are able to establish yourself in the state of perfect *shinay* right now. You will not be able to, and if you expect to, you will be disappointed. One should accept meditation as it is presently: with or without clarity, with or without thoughts. What matters is to meditate and to persevere.

QUESTIONS AND ANSWERS

Question: What is the effect on meditation of keeping the eyes open rather than closed?

Answer: If one has a general tendency to be agitated, it is better to close the eyes. If, on the other hand, one has a tendency to be sleepy, it is better to keep the eyes widely open.

Question: What can be done concerning impatience? One finds, for instance, the meditation is a little too long and thoughts on this subject begin to arise.

Answer: Yes, this is what happens when one is a beginner. This is why it is preferable to meditate for very short periods of time, and to do many brief sessions.

Question: What causes sleepiness?

Answer: Generally, it is the fact that we have created in our past lives a *karma* that leads to sleepiness. This is why we now have this tendency. However, sleepiness can also come from a poor state of health, or from a great physical fatigue.

Question: When one keeps one's eyes open, should things outside remain distinct? Is it sleepiness if they become unclear?

Answer: In the methods we have just seen (e.g., breathing, the *tigle* at the level of the forehead or the Buddha in the heart) if one sees these supports clearly and does not see the external world anymore, it is not sleepiness. But if the external is unclear, and one does not see clearly the meditation support, this then is sleepiness.

Question: If, during meditation, one feels an impression of great warmth, what is this and what should one do about it?

Answer: When one places the mind on itself, this warmth is the sign that there is a certain perception of the ultimate nature of the mind. When one is a beginner, this experience of warmth may sometimes happen, but it is in fact of no importance.

Question: Is it necessary to practice successively the different methods that have been explained, or is it better to choose only one?

Answer: It is preferable, initially, to practice them

- 83 -

successively. Then, if you see that one suits you better than the others, you remain with this one.

Question: What can one do to counter sleepiness when tensing the mind is not sufficient to overcome it?

Answer: When one has a strong tendency to sleep, one has to verify whether the meditation posture is correct, in particular that one's back is very straight. Secondly, one has to tense one's mind slightly. Finally, one imagines that there is a small white *tigle* in one's heart and that it is undifferentiated from one's mind. This *tigle* rises, following the body's axis, exits from the crown of one's head, then goes up very high into the sky. One imagines that it arrives in a very bright and clear space. One maintains this visualization for a moment, then one thinks that one becomes one with the sky itself.

These different methods will allow one to find a remedy to sleepiness when it occurs during meditation. However, one should also attempt to act on the deep cause of it. To dissipate the karmic veils which provoke sleepiness, one can do the practice of *Dorje Sempa*[1] and make offerings of light.

Question: Now what would be the antidote to great agitation?

Answer: When one has a lot of thoughts, it indicates that our mind is turned toward the things of this world. One thinks about material goods, about what one is going to eat, about friends, about places that are dear to one, about what one likes and does not like. Since our thoughts are directed toward that which makes up the world around us, it is necessary to understand that this world does not

---

[1]*Dorje Sempa:* see page 63.

entirely deserve the interest that one places in it. First of all, impermanent and devoid of stability, all phenomena change from instant to instant. Since this world is transitory, a strong attachment to it has no foundation. Secondly, phenomena are by nature suffering. Through impermanence that which is agreeable can become disagreeable, as, for instance a good meal that results in a feeling of heaviness and a stomachache. Finally, phenomena do not have self-existence because they are only an illusory creation. If we are conscious of these three facts we will be less attracted by the world, and we will have fewer thoughts.

Given that agitation is also the product of karmic veils, here again, the practice of *Dorje Sempa*, and offerings will aid us.

While meditating, in order to remedy agitation, one relaxes physically and looks down. One can also imagine that there is a black *tigle* in one's heart that descends and loses itself in the depths of the earth.

Practicing *shinay* correctly will make us feel very good inside, relaxed and alert.

City dwellers like to leave on weekends. They think that this will give them a break from their work during the week. Friday night, they are very happy thinking that they will go to the countryside or the seashore for two days. But Saturday morning, difficulties begin. One has to prepare what is necessary, look for things one cannot find when needed, and hurry. Then one gets on the road and finds oneself in a traffic jam with the various annoyances of the traffic. One must be attentive, look out for the police, and so on. Once one has arrived at the destination, one must worry about what to eat and where to sleep. Sunday night, one gets on the road again, finds the same traffic jams, gets irritated and finishes the weekend exhausted.

When one practices *shinay*, one finds true rest, one takes a true vacation.

Question: Since the nature of the mind is not an object one can look at, how can one turn oneself toward the essence of the mind to look at it?

Answer: At the beginning, one may think likewise, but when you have meditated a lot, you will understand.

Question: Can one work with sounds rather than on visualizations?

Answer: One can also focus on sounds to settle one's attention without distraction. One could also concentrate on smells, for instance those which emanate from incense.

Question: All kinds of sounds reach us. Is it necessary to accept all of them, or should we be selective?

Answer: One can concentrate on the totality of the perceived sounds. In particular, in the first experiences of meditation, one tends to consider the noise as an annoyance which risks irritating us. In this case, it is a good solution to use these sounds as supports. They will automatically cease to be harmful. For the people who live in the city, this method is very beneficial.

Question: Can one practice shinay before sleeping?

Answer: Yes, of course, it is very good. One can, for instance, practice *shinay* ten minutes before going to bed and ten minutes when one wakes up.

Question: Rinpoche has said that a good practice of shinay must be "open, clear and stable." What exactly does "open" mean? Does it mean a mind that can peacefully accept all that happens?

Answer: "Open" means a mind that does not impose

difficulties upon itself, that is happy, that experiences a feeling of ease. It is not to be like a person who is carrying a heavy weight, but like one who has dropped a heavy weight. Meditating with effort, with a tension of the will is meditating with a heavy weight on your back. One meditates, but it is very difficult because body and mind are tense. When one meditates with effort, one carries meditation like a weight. If during meditation one has an impression of inner difficulty and lack of ease, it is a sign that the meditator is in this situation. When one "puts down the weight," one experiences by contrast a sensation of comfort, a pleasant feeling.

The perfect practice of *shinay* possesses fully these three qualities: stability, clarity and openness. For beginners they are not always present. It is necessary to be conscious of the difficulties in our meditation and consequently find a remedy, exactly as the person who sails has to deal with the wind in order to sail forward.

Eyes and chin during meditation

Meditation mudra

Bodhisattva posture

Adamantine posture

Superior Vision– "Lhatong"

The immense multiplicity of possibilities for manifestation implies an extreme variety of types of existence, each having its own determinants. We human beings are endowed with intelligence and are able to express ourselves with the aid of a complex and extensive system of symbols. We are capable of understanding, and are endowed with an intellect much superior to that of animals. Being conscious of this favorable existential situation is a legitimate cause to rejoice. However, we must recognize the obvious limit of it, which is suffering. Physically and mentally, we suffer.

Many people have a completely erroneous idea of the relationship uniting body and mind. They think that the mind is a totally dependant function of the physical organism. For them, in the absence of a body, there is no mind. The death of the physical body would subsequently mean the simultaneous end of the mind. Contrary to these materialistic views, spiritual knowledge teaches us that body and mind are not linked in an indissoluble relationship. The body is a product which stems from genetic and physical elements of the parents but the mind does not come from the parents' minds. It has existed, in the domain of conditioned existence since time without beginning as individualized consciousness, immaterial and continuous. Body and mind are essentially distinct.

Suffering affects our body and our mind. Physical suffering is only occasional, caused by sickness or temporary circumstances. Mental suffering is a continual state and remains with us day and night, however, we are rarely conscious of it as force of habit makes us accept it as normal. Let us suppose that someone finds him or herself in the best of possible physical circumstances: in good health, replete, comfortably resting at home at night. However, as long as he or she has not sunk into sleep, the mind is not at peace as this person continues to turn over events of the day or recent past, or worries about future, nourishing projects, hopes and fears. Even when asleep, this individual's sleep is troubled by unconscious imprints of his or her mind expressed as dreams which are often as full of worries as during wakefulness. In the morning, as soon as he or she is awake, preoccupations of the day come to enter the mind.

Outer circumstances are not sufficient to assure inner happiness. Eliminating mental suffering is, in fact, much more important than eliminating the apparent causes of outer suffering. But we are mistaken in our objective. Thinking we will attain happiness, we continually embark on an attempt to reorganize the world around us, but to no avail. Material goods and external objects, far from being able to free us from inner suffering, are most often causes that greatly increase it. The true means to liberate oneself from inner suffering is the practice of *mahamudra* meditation through which the natural and genuine state of the mind is uncovered. Two steps are necessary: mental calming (*shinay*) and the superior vision (*lhatong*).

Our mind is generally occupied with an unceasing production of thoughts, similar to boiling water. Meditating in order to pacify this boiling and then remaining in a stable state without tension is referred to as mental calming. Superior vision involves the process of recognizing the nature of the mind. Whether for mental calming or superior vision, it is, in any case, essential to know first how to place one's mind: relaxed, open, and without any mental superimposition. Let us suppose that a person is getting ready to watch a show and is standing up with a heavy load on his or her shoulders. This person may see the show very well but the load on his or her back is too great a handicap to allow him or her to fully appreciate the performance. Another person, on the other hand, puts down the burden, sits comfortably in an armchair and enjoys the performance without difficulty. Both spectators are able to see the show. But in the first case, the person's mind is subject to two contradictory stimuli: on one hand, watching the performance, and on the other the discomfort of the load on the back. When we wish to meditate, if we keep the mind contracted and do not establish a state of spacious relaxation, we will be pulled in two opposing directions: tension and worry on one side, and the object of meditation on the other. The second viewer, having put down the load, and along with it the discomfort, can pay full attention to the performance. Approaching meditation with a relaxed and open mind, we can similarly devote ourselves fully and without difficulty to the object of meditation, our mind being occupied by one thing only.

The cornerstone of any meditation is to know how to place one's mind in this manner. It is said in one manual:

Good relaxation: good meditation
Mediocre relaxation: mediocre meditation
Bad relaxation: bad meditation.

Which degree of relaxation would be the best? It is true that excessive relaxation predisposes the mind toward distraction and dispersion. Without falling into this excess, one must make an effort to find the threshold of maximum effective relaxation. Abandoning all vigilance would lead to a collapse into confusion. One must maintain vigilance, however, with as little tension as possible.

Some people attempt to block all thoughts while meditating. They fight so that nothing other than the object of concentration occupies their mind. Others establish themselves in a state characterized by a kind of absence of consciousness, a deep and unintelligent obscurity. These two attitudes are in opposition to meditation.

Mental calming implies as much clarity as possible, allied with a deep feeling of freedom. When we contemplate the sea during the day we can see stones and seaweed deep down through the clear water. Our meditation should have this same clarity, which allows us to be fully conscious of the present situation. At night, on the other hand, the surface of the water is dark and opaque, a massive shape, which does not allow our vision to penetrate it. In the same manner, a thick and gloomy mind, in spite of its appearance of stability, prevents meditation.

DISTINCTION BETWEEN SHINAY AND LHATONG

Mental calming quiets and stabilizes the mind, but the true mind's nature is not recognized. We still do not understand what it is and the fundamental questions remain unanswered, or as merely intellectual assumptions. Superior vision goes further. The mind calmed, superior vision recognizes its own essence without uncertainty. It leads to a direct and discernable experience. Because it represents a higher level of comprehension than the simple calm of the mind, one calls it superior vision.

Both mental calming and superior vision focus on the mind. The object of focus, the mind, is identical, but the manner of seeing is different. At night the moon reflects on the surface of a container full of water. When the container is agitated, one cannot perceive the shape of the moon but only sees a simple and confused luminosity. If tho container is left to rest, the surface of the water becomes gradually calm and smooth. This corresponds to the phase of mental pacification through which the mind gets rid of the agitation of thoughts. When the water is perfectly calm, one can see clearly that which is reflected and recognize the perceived shape for what it actually is. When the mind has been similarly quieted through the exercise of mental calming, then superior vision allows us to recognize its nature.

THE PRACTICE OF LHATONG

First we assume the correct bodily posture without tension, then we place our mind in the state of *shinay*, open and relaxed. We taste thus an experience of calm mixed with a feeling of well-being. Now let us investigate where this calm mind resides. Is it in our head, in a determined place within our body, or in the body as a whole? In our heart? In our brain? What is the essence of this calm mind? Where does it dwell? Let us examine this carefully.

(*meditation*)

The unfruitful character of the investigation leads us to discover the non-localization of the calm mind through our own experience. Wherever we looked for it, it was not to be found. It was nowhere. We will now give up the examination and resume *shinay* as before.

(*meditation*)

The investigation did not allow us to discover the mind wherever it exists. However, leaving our mind at rest, we really have the feeling that a mind at rest exists; a feeling of happiness, calm, of something that exists, a sense of being. When we do not proceed with an examination, we experience the existence of this calm mind. When we then look at the essence of this calm mind, we cannot in any way say "it is this" or "it is that." We are totally incapable of describing what it is because we are unable to find anything we could call "a calm mind." If, however, we were to conclude that this calm mind does not exist at all, we would be contradicting the feeling of being which we experience while our mind is at rest. We are led to the discovery of a state of inexpressible being. Recognizing this and directly experiencing it, is what is referred to as *lhatong*, the superior vision[1].

This recognition is still possible through the alternation of rest and examination. Once a certain level of experience with meditation is attained, these two states are no longer dissociated, and the exercise of alternation becomes superfluous. Reaching this non-separation of the calm mind and the investigating mind is superior vision in the fullest meaning of the term. Nevertheless, proceeding by alternation is a first approach.

Now we can all see the stairs lighted by the lamp. Let us look at them and generate in our mind the image of these stairs.

(meditation)

---

[1]For the uninformed person, the method just presented and the subsequent conclusions may seem very simplistic and indirect in order to arrive at some truisms. Whether we are conscious of it or not, the experience we have of our mind is extremely localized and reified. The method explained here, if followed without prejudgment, perseverance and referral to the explanations of a qualified instructor, has as its goal the progressive dissolution of the illusory crystallization with which we are fixated. The same comment is valid for the second exercise, explained in the following pages.

The thought of the stairs is now present in our mind. Where does this thought arise? What location does it come from? What is its source?

(*meditation*)

Examining the origin of this thought, we cannot say that it comes from outside, nor can we discover its source inside our physical organism. The thought of the stairs was not introduced into our mind in the manner of a person coming from outside, into a room. It is there without having come from anywhere.

(*meditation*)

We are powerless to find any origin for this thought.

Now, when the thought of the stairs is present in our mind, where does it dwell? Here? There? Outside or inside of our body? Let us carefully examine this. When a person enters the room, he or she comes from outside, crosses the threshold then remains in a limited and defined location, the room. Can we, in a similar fashion, identify a limited and defined location where the thought dwells?

(*meditation*)

What form does it have, not the mentally perceived image, but the thought itself? What is its shape, size? Can we see it? Our investigation emerges once again without finding anything.

Let us now look carefully at these flowers.

(*meditation*)

Is the thought of the stairs still in your mind at the

same time as it is occupied looking at the flowers? When the thought of the stairs ceased, how did it go?

When the thought of the stairs formed in our mind, we asked ourselves if it was like a person entering a room through the door and then remaining inside. When the thought of the stairs ceased, replaced by the thought of the flowers, how did it go? Is it like leaving a room to go somewhere else?

(*meditation*)

Where does the thought of flowers come from? Let us now look at this statue. Is the thought of the flowers still there? Where has it gone?

(*meditation*)

Examining where the thought came from, we were unable to find its origin. Searching for its localization, once present, we could not apprehend it; and, when it had ceased, we could not discover where it had gone.

Thoughts do not come from anywhere, do not remain anywhere and do not go anywhere. They do not exist by themselves.

THE EXAMPLE OF THE STUFFED TIGER

As long as we do not know the nature of the mind, we live with the conviction that thoughts really exist. Taken as real, they become the cause of suffering. One sees some people so tormented by a thought that they cease to eat, becoming thin and pale, with hollow expressionless eyes. These physical repercussions illustrate well the force of these thoughts when they are taken as real.

One sees children's stuffed animals, which

sometimes look real. Tigers, lions and leopards have wide open jaws, threatening fangs and fix their prey with fighting eyes. Any little child can be frightened by a stuffed tiger, as he or she believes he or she is in the presence of a real threat. His or her mistake is the unique cause of his or her suffering. Thus, where there is no real tiger, the child believes there is one. On the other hand, the same child may be very happy with a stuffed horse, according it a real existence, and investing it with the kindness and gentleness of a genuine horse. Not recognizing the nature of our thoughts, we are similar to this little child. We take as real something that is not, and from there we feel suffering or joy.

On the other hand, the meditator who achieves *mahamudra*, recognizing the true nature of his or her mind, is comparable to an adult who would not be misled by an imitation of a tiger or a horse. The adult would think, "It is so well made, one would think it is a real tiger, or one would think it is a horse." But he or she does not mistake the reality of the object, and is not led to react as he or she would in the presence of a true tiger or true horse. He or she is free of the fears and joys which would be present in a real situation. Similarly, for the one who has realized *mahamudra*, thoughts from which the real character is uncovered will not give rise to emotional complications. They engender neither suffering nor joy[1].

All kinds of thoughts and images appear in our mind, but they do not have any real existence. *Lhatong*

---

[1] It does not mean at all that the mind dwells from then on in a state of permanent, boring and dull indifference. On the contrary, the mind experiences its own joy which has no common measure with ordinary joys. It is beyond the concepts of joy and non-joy. The mind of a liberated being is not only beyond suffering, it is by nature, and in an inalterable way, peace, lucidity, intelligence, happiness, love and power. It is infinitely more alive than we are.

recognizes simultaneously the mental manifestations, and their absence of inherent existence. This does not mean that one should attempt to erase the manifestation, to deny the creative faculty of the mind, rather one should see its character devoid of self-existence. A false tiger does not appear with less "form," it is the aspect of manifestation. Knowing that it is not real corresponds to the aspect of vacuity. Superior vision recognizes the form of the tiger and its unreality, the union of manifestation and vacuity at the same time.

TAKING THE REMEDY

As many methods exist for practicing *lhatong*, as for practicing *shinay*. We have already seen two approaches here:
- analyzing the nature of the calm mind,
- determining where thoughts come from, where they dwell, where they go.

It is not sufficient to understand them intellectually. One must put them into practice though meditation. Not meditating and being content with thinking that what we have said is correct would be sterile. When we are sick, the physician diagnoses the illness, prescribes medication and explains the expected effects. However, we will not get well if we content ourselves with the diagnosis, with having understood which medicines to take, how to take them, and the expected result. It is necessary to take the prescribed medicines in order to recover. In the same manner, it is not sufficient to understand what meditation is; one should meditate.

Meditating for a few days, a few months, or even a year and then giving up, would not be fruitful either. A sick person has to take medicine until he or she is completely well. If this person stops taking the medication during treatment, even if the latter has lasted for months or years, the illness will again take over. We must similarly pursue our meditation until we have attained an effective and stable realization. Regularity and perseverance are the two necessary conditions for beneficial meditation.

MESSAGE TO THE PEOPLE OF PROVENCE

For several years an aged *lama*, called Lama Gelek[1] resided in Aix-en-Provence. He sowed the seeds of devotion in the heart of many fortunate disciples. The instructions I have given to you over the past few days are water and fertilizer I have poured on this seed. I have great hope that a few years from now, the plant will bear the beautiful fruit of authentic experience and realization. If you are able to eat this fruit, taste the flavor and nectar, it will be of immense benefit to you as well as to others.

---

[1]Lama Gelek resided in Aix-en-Provence from 1977 to 1980 where Kalu Rinpoche had given him charge of the Tibetan center located then on *Rue de la Fourane*. As a young monk, he was noticed by his master, Sangye Tulku, who transmitted numerous teachings to him privately, even at night when he would sometimes call him to come into his room. Lama Gelek then spent the major part of his life in retreat, until he went into exile at the end of the fifties. In India he met with Kalu Rinpoche and again did a three year retreat at Sonada Monastery at the same time as Bokar Rinpoche. It was also in Sonada that he passed away, in July 1981, following a devastating illness. The wonderful signs which accompanied his death confirm the deep realization acquired during his life.

Dorje Sempa

Question: Where do conflicting emotions come from?

Answer: Since time without beginning, our mind has been in the grip of the ego. Furthermore, during the succession of our lives, unconscious imprints have been formed and condition our perception of the world and emotional reaction to any situation. Anger, desire, and so on, are parts of these imprints. This is where conflicting emotions come from.

When these emotions arise strongly in our mind, the remedy is not to repress them. Recognizing the presence and strength of emotion, it is without doubt preferable to say, "Welcome, welcome, do come in!" Perhaps the emotion will shy away from our invitation!

The constraining character of a thought or an emotion comes from the fact that we identify with it. If, on the other hand, we leave it without owner, without occupant, it will stop being harmful. Thoughts are like cars on a road: when an accident occurs and if we are not in the car, we are safe!

Question: What should one do when facing difficulties visualizing?

Answer: Visualization is difficult when one begins. *Taking Refuge*, practicing *Dorje Sempa* and *Guru Yoga*, and our own perseverance are means by which we can gradually eliminate the difficulty. In our mind, numerous thoughts arise, linked with the conflicting emotions, anger, and others. Even if we have understood that they have no self-existence, that they do not really exist, and that they are harmful, thoughts appear independently of our will. This is why it is necessary to purify our mind from the faults and veils that affect it through the practice of *Dorje Sempa* and to unite our mind to the mind of our teacher.

Question: How do you pray to the lama?

Answer: While visualizing the *lama*, we think that he or she is truly present and we trust ourselves to the *lama's* protection. We ask that our suffering be pushed aside, and that the veils which obscure our mind be dissipated; that our mind find peace and happiness. If we know the prayer of *Refuge*, we can use it in this way; if not, we can also pray with our own words.

Question: How can we determine the difference between that which comes from our ego and that which comes from our pure nature?

Answer: Our mind is simultaneously knowledge and ignorance. Generally, thoughts of a dualistic nature come from the ignorant aspect, while the primordial non-dual consciousness is the expression of knowledge. However, faith, compassion, and so on, are also expressions of knowledge.

Question: What should one do about a problem which comes back again and again?

Answer: The resurgence of a problem comes from *karma*, from certain veils and faults which obscure the mind. The remedy is, therefore, to purify oneself through the practice of *Dorje Sempa, shinay, lhatong,* by the devotion to the *lama*, *taking Refuge,* and having compassion for all beings. Once the negative *karma* is dissipated, the problem will not be able to present itself again because its cause will have disappeared.

Our mind is imprisoned by the knots of ego,

conflicting emotions and suffering. Praying to the *lama*, practicing *Dorje Sempa*, and uniting one's mind to the *lama's* mind allow one to release this grip and recover a state of relaxation and ease. This will greatly reinforce our trust in the *dharma*, and will promote the spontaneous rise of compassion toward those who, deprived of the *dharma*, do not know the nature of their mind.

Question: Where does one place the meditation of Chenrezig in relation to shinay and lhatong?

Answer: The meditation of Chenrezig includes both *shinay* and *lhatong*. When we visualize Chenrezig above our head, imagining his face, arms, ornaments, and so on, we place our mind without distraction on this appearance; that is *shinay*. When we simultaneously understand that this form of Chenrezig is non-material, does not exist as a "thing," is similar to a mirror, although at the same time is not inert but is wisdom, love and strength, that is *lhatong*. A good meditation of Chenrezig encompasses both *shinay* and *lhatong*.

Dorje Sempa

Further Information on the Superior Vision-"Lhatong"

When one observes one's mind, one cannot find a place where one's thoughts originate, neither can one discover a place where they dwell, nor a place where they go when they disappear. This is an indication that thoughts are not "things," that they are not real.

However, since we do not know the nature of the mind, we grasp at thoughts as if they were "things" that truly exist and, consequently, we suffer.

Although thoughts are devoid of reality, they still arise in our mind. They are the product of extensive conditioning which engenders their manifestation. How does this conditioning take shape in our mind? It happens in the same way as our daily activities leave imprints in our mind which later surface in our dreams.

Our thoughts, devoid of reality, are similar to mirages which heat makes appear in the desert. Seen from far away, a mirage seems real. Nevertheless it has no reality. One cannot say that it comes from somewhere, that it dwells somewhere, nor can one say that when it disappears it goes somewhere. However, to unmask its appearance of reality, one must examine it to become aware that it is nothing but an illusory appearance. The same is true for thoughts: one must understand that they are not real and this understanding will diminish our suffering.

Seeing that thoughts are devoid of self-existence is what one calls *lhatong*, the "superior vision."

Generally, before practicing *lhatong*, one first practices *shinay* in order to reduce the inner agitation. If one approaches *lhatong* directly, one risks increasing the production of thoughts. This is why, one must first establish a good base of *shinay*. Nevertheless, when one experiences a lot of internal suffering, the practice of *lhatong* will help us.

THE PRACTICE OF LHATONG

Just as for the practice of *shinay*, we will find it of great help to first address a prayer to our spiritual teacher who we imagine present, seated on a luminous lotus above our head. At the end of this prayer he or she merges with us and we consider that we have received his or her grace.

First exercise

Comfortably at ease in the seven point posture, we begin to practice *shinay* as before, focusing our attention on our breathing. We breathe naturally and consider that our breathing and our mind are one.

Once our mind is focused without distraction on our breathing, we ask ourselves what color is the breath we feel passing within our body, what shape is it, what is its size and its essence. Meditation which proceeds to this analysis is *lhatong*.

Second exercise

Again, we practice *shinay*, this time concentrating on a white *tigle* within our forehead. *Tigle* and mind are undifferentiated. Now we analyze the presence of this *tigle*: what is its essence? Did it come from inside or outside of the body? Is it a production of our forehead? While this *tigle* continues to be clearly perceived, where is it? Is it inside or outside the forehead or somewhere in between? When it disappears, where does it go?

Proceeding in this manner to an examination of the origin, localization and disappearance of the *tigle*, it is very unlikely that you found any answers. You undoubtedly arrived at the conclusion that there is nothing identifiable as a truly existing object, nothing that could be found. In this case it would be useless to pursue additional analysis. One simply rests from then on in this state where nothing can be found: this is *lhatong*.

Third exercise

We first practice *shinay* visualizing Buddha Sakyamuni in our heart as support. We then ask ourselves what is the nature of this clearly perceived Buddha. Is he made of cloth like a *tangka*[1], or of clay or metal like a statue? From where did he appear, inside our body or outside? While present, where is he? When he disappears, where does he go? One asks the same questions as in the previous exercise. One may think that it is useless to ask these questions again since one just did this for the *tigle*. This would be a mistake. If one does not proceed to analysis, one cannot experience it. In fact it is this experience that is of importance.

Here again, the result of the examination will be that one was not able to find anything.

---

[1]*Tangka*: painting on cloth that represents sacred images.

- 115 -

For those who know how to meditate as we have just seen, it is a very agreeable experience, like a kind of grand spectacle that unfolds. If, on the contrary, one tries without achieving a satisfactory experience, it can be dismaying and tiring.

When giving instructions on meditation, normally one explains *shinay* first and approaches *lhatong* only after a certain mental stability has been acquired. In Tibet the teacher always proceeded in this fashion in two stages, to avoid the risk that premature instructions in *lhatong* may lead to an increase of thoughts in a unprepared mind. In the West, because of the circumstances, it is not always possible to follow this principle. The general rules concerning the two approaches are therefore given simultaneously. Neither the teacher nor the student can do otherwise. It is therefore, for the meditator to see which is the most beneficial for him or her. If you have a certain stability of mind and are rarely carried away by thoughts, you can do *lhatong*. If on the contrary you notice a lot of agitation, it will be better to apply yourself to the practice of *shinay*.

The important thing is to study one's own meditation, and see what occurs in one's mind. If the teacher gives many explanations and if the student spends a lot of time listening to them, it is not really useful. Without the experience of the meditation itself, instructions are fruitless. Even if a teacher and a student stayed together for a hundred years, with the teacher explaining meditation for a hundred years and the student listening carefully, taking notes and thinking about it for a hundred years, very little inner experience could be obtained.

Suppose you want to learn to pilot a plane. You could find an instructor who would first explain the theory of aviation, the functions of the various instruments and switches, and the significance of the indicators. You would first write these explanations in a notebook, then learn the names, descriptions and functions [of the aircraft and its instrumentation]. However, as long as you have not been effectively at the controls, and have not learned the responses of the aircraft through your own experience, you will not know how to fly at all. Once you are in the aircraft, and are told to operate the controls to take on fuel, take off, change directions, and land, then you develop a direct experience of what happens when you actually perform that which has been explained to you. You really learn to pilot a plane beyond a simple intellectual understanding.

In my case, for instance, I do not know how to drive a car. If I wanted to learn and you just described the functioning of the vehicle to me—that engaging a lever in a certain manner would make the car go forward or in reverse, depressing this pedal or another causes the car to accelerate or to brake, pushing this button turns on the headlights and so on—I would never know how to drive. Whereas, if you place me at the steering wheel and have me do everything you have explained to me, an experience is engraved in my mind which will allow me to genuinely learn.

It is the same with meditation, even if it is necessary to receive some instruction at first, the important thing is to develop an inner understanding by meditating. It is then that we will be able to uncover that which is truly our own mind.

To practice *lhatong*, we need to follow the path that establishes our mind in a state of peaceful stability. Then, we must try to determine wherein dwells the calm mind. Is it outside of our body, inside or somewhere in between? What is its shape, its size, what color is it? We proceed first with this analysis, at the end of which we find neither place, shape, size nor color. Then, we rest in this state in which nothing has been found.

We saw how to apply this method using three supports. We must understand clearly, however, that *lhatong* is not limited to the analysis; rather, it resides in actually abiding in the experience obtained at the end of the analysis.

Continually repeating the process of examination would not make a lot of sense. This would consist in looking at something, discovering that there is nothing, looking again and discovering again that there is nothing, and so on. In truth, one looks only until one makes the discovery that there is nothing to be found; then one abides in this state where nothing is found.

Not carrying out the analysis at all would be just as much an error as pursuing it without stopping. Let us imagine a farmer who has lost a cow. He could think that it might have gotten lost at one place or another, or he may decide that it is definitively lost and say, "There is no point in looking for it." If he thinks the latter, he may be able to sustain this idea for a moment, but before long some doubts will sprout in his mind. He will not be able to refrain from thinking, "Yes, maybe it is lost for good but it might be at one place or another . . . . " In order to rid himself of the doubt definitively, he will be compelled to search for the cow, to go to the forest, the hollows, the groves where it might have found shelter, and verify with his own eyes that it is not there. If after a thorough search the cow has not been discovered, the farmer, when he is back home, will not have anymore doubt. He knows *from experience* that the animal is really lost. He does not think anymore that the cow must be here or there. If he were to continue to look for it after he is perfectly sure that the cow cannot be found, his action would be pointless.

It is the same thing in the case of our mind. We now live within the conception, "I have a mind," in other words, in the belief that our mind exists as a thing. The teacher tells us, "In reality, the mind does not exist as a thing." If we accept this simply because our teacher has told us it is like this, it is very probable that doubts will remain deep within us. We will think that it is very likely true since the teacher said it, but it will not be a certainty for us. If, on another hand, we proceed with an analysis that allows us to verify for ourselves that the mind cannot be grasped as a self-existing object, no more doubts will remain. The belief in the objective reality of our mind will be erased through the evidence obtained by direct experience. Pursuing the analysis further when the evidence has already been obtained would make no more sense than to continue to look for the cow when it has become clear that it is nowhere to be found.

BEYOND WORDS

Instructions for practicing *shinay* and *lhatong* are given with the help of words. However, it is the blessing of the teacher and our own meditation that will lead to true experience and understanding. Words in themselves will always be insufficient. One must put the instructions received into practice, even if one cannot devote a lot of time to them. Simply acquiring the knowledge of them would not be of any use, as interesting as it might seem.

Question: One could think that there never was a cow, but also that the cow has always been there.

Answer: If one had not lost the cow, one would not feel the need to look for it. But this is only an example.

When one says that the mind does not exist, we mean that the mind does not exist as a material thing with a form, limits and characteristics which can be defined by the senses. This does not mean that the mind does not exist at all.

Question: While doing shinay meditation, I felt very tense but much more relaxed when we did lhatong. However, it seems to me it was said that one must practice the first step before approaching the second one. Is it necessary then to persevere when one is tense or what should one do?

Answer: You can pursue the meditation in which you feel relaxed, even if it is devoid of an object of visualization.

Question: I do not see the difference between, on one hand, shinay without thought, and on another, the state in which one rests when nothing has been found at the end of the analysis of lhatong.

Answer: The difference is the following: in *shinay* one simply remains in a clear and thoughtless state, while in *lhatong* the analysis leads to the recognition that there is no "I" in our mind, contrary to the belief anchored in ourselves. The state in which one remains then is one where there is no "I."

When we begin, we first practice *shinay* from which one uncovers an inner experience. Then, one practices *lhatong* which allows one to develop another type of experience. We cannot do both simultaneously. When our practice deepens, *shinay* and *lhatong* become indivisible.

Question: Does the experience of the state where one does not find anything act as a revelation, as a very strong impression?

Answer: At the beginning the experience of finding nothing is simply finding nothing, something very ordinary. Progressively, through the development of meditation, it becomes a more and more powerful experience.

Question: Why is our mind tense?

Answer: There are profound reasons for the tension of our mind. We perceive the five objects of the senses, (i.e., forms, sounds, smells, tastes and objects of touch) as exterior to ourselves. Inside, an "I" perceives these objects. Therefore, there is duality, and between the two poles of this duality, thoughts of attachment and repulsion are created. It is these thoughts in very great profusion that keep our mind from being relaxed.

In truth, however, the external objects that our senses perceive do not have any self-existence. They are not endowed with the independent existence we attribute to them, but are only illusory projections of our own mind. If one develops an understanding of what the external objects really are, our mind relaxes.

One may think there is something strange here: these objects, we see them, hear them, smell them, taste them and touch them. How can we say they do not exist? In fact, if they appear endowed with a real external and independent existence, this is due to fundamental ignorance, as well as latent conditioning which has formed in our mind since time without beginning.

It is the same process as that which controls our dreams: at night conditioned phenomena appear because of that which we have done and thought during the day.

Nevertheless you will say, if I knock on this table there is really something solid against which my hand clashes. How is this possible since nothing really exists? This grasping of reality comes from the deep conditioning that exerts a great constraint on our mind in such a manner that a simple and intellectual understanding is not sufficient to undo the mechanism. This conditioning continues to make us accept as real that which is not.

Suppose I have jaundice. I would then have the tendency to see everything colored yellow. This white glass I would perceive as yellow. Someone in good health would tell me, "Oh, no, it is not yellow, it is white." And the person would explain to me that my illness has created an illusion which modifies colors and does not permit me to see them as they really are. Since everybody would say the same thing, I would accept that the glass is white. But it would only be an intellectual approbation which, as long as I have not been cured, would not prevent me from seeing as yellow that which is not yellow. Similarly for all phenomena, understanding that they are illusionary is not sufficient to go beyond this illusion.

In order for the illusion of yellow created by the jaundice to cease, I must see a physician who will give me the appropriate medicine. If I follow the treatment, I will progressively feel the effects and the symptoms of the sickness will decrease. I would see less and less yellow, up to the point that upon complete recovery, I would no longer perceive as yellow that which is not yellow.

Permeating oneself with the idea that phenomena do not have any real existence, will not prevent me from feeling pain if I smack this table very hard, illusory as it is. In order for the illusion to cease, I must take the remedy, that is to say follow the instructions given by the teacher. Through practice of these instructions, grasping at a reality in phenomena will effectively diminish.

Let us come back to the tension of the mind during meditation. When one holds the mind without constraint, without doing anything, it remains relaxed naturally. If tension occurs, one should remain within this tension and it will disappear by itself.

Vajradhara Buddha

The Legs, Head and Body of Mahamudra

The *mahamudra*[1] is a term which designates the mode of being, the ultimate nature, of all beings.

What fundamentally is this mind that characterizes beings? Is it within the body? Is it outside of the body? Or is it somewhere in between? Is it white, red, or of another color? What is its shape? What are its dimensions?

If we examine the mind carefully, we ascertain that it is empty by nature. One cannot assign any material characteristic to it.

The mind is empty; it is not a thing. Does this mean that it is nothing? No. The mind cannot be simple emptiness, simple nothingness, since according to our experience, it is the basis from which the multiple thoughts of conditioned existence appear. From it arise anger and other conflicting emotions on the negative side, and faith and compassion on the positive. This natural production of thoughts is sufficient to demonstrate that it is not only emptiness. When one looks for the mode of being of the

---

[1]The term *mahamudra* designates both the ultimate nature of the mind and the meditation which leads to recognition of it, and of which *shinay* and *lhatong* are the steps. It refers, therefore, to the highest level of practice.

mind and asks what it is, one cannot, in fact, elicit any answer. One cannot say that it is something. If one were to conclude that it is nothing at all, one would also have to admit that this conclusion is not relevant since there are feelings of happiness and suffering. Thus, the mind cannot be defined by the notions of existence and non-existence[1].

In truth, if the nature of the mind is inexpressible, it is because it is the *dharmakaya*, the Absolute Body. However this *dharmakaya* is beyond the field of ordinary thinking, beyond that which can be expressed in words, and beyond any concept. Nevertheless, although the *dharmakaya* is our true nature we do not recognize it, and we wander in *samsara*, the cycle of existence and suffering. Recognizing the *dharmakaya* is the function of the *dharma* and especially of *mahamudra* meditation.

THE SOURCE OF THE PRACTICE

In the *Kagyupa* lineage, the practice of *mahamudra* was revealed at the source, by the primordial Buddha Vajradhara to the great accomplished Indian master Tilopa who, having obtained ultimate realization, transmitted it to Naropa. From Naropa, it passed to Marpa the Translator, then to Milarepa, then Gampopa who transmitted it to Tusum Kyenpa, the First Karmapa. The tradition was then

---

[1]The notions of existence and non-existence applied to our mind may seem difficult to grasp. The difficulty may be increased due to our implicit belief that our mind is a product of the brain, whereas Buddhism considers the brain as a temporary support for the function of the mind. These notions constitute the "view," that is to say, the theoretical foundation upon which the practice of meditation relies. Long and subtle development is necessary in order to support this view. Bokar Rinpoche gives here only the essentials in order to permit us to better understand meditation.

held by the succession of Karmapas, without interruption and in its totality.

I, myself, received this transmission of the grace of *mahamudra* from my *source lamas*, the Sixteenth Karmapa and Kalu Rinpoche[1].

A COMPLETE BODY

To be complete, the practice of *mahamudra* must join three elements that can be compared to the parts of a body; the absence of one or another will prevent the whole from functioning. One says that:
- non-attachment is the legs of *mahamudra*;
- devotion is the head;
- meditation is the trunk or body.

A body is functional only if it is complete. A body without a head would be useless, as would a body without a trunk. A body which had a head and trunk, but was without legs would not be able to accomplish the activities of a complete body. A body, to completely fulfill its functions, must possess the integrity of its parts. In the same way, in order for the practice of *mahamudra* to be effective it must be complete: head, legs and trunk. If any of these are missing, it will not be genuine *mahamudra*.

---

[1]From the masters of the lineage mentioned here the first two are Indian and the others Tibetan.
- Tilopa: 988-1069;
- Naropa: 1016-1100;
- Marpa: 1012-1097;
- Milarepa: 1040-1123;
- Gampopa: 1079-1153;
- Tusum Kyenpa: 1110-1193;
- Sixteenth Karmapa: 1924-1981;
- Kalu Rinpoche: 1904-1989.

When one is in the grip of a very strong attachment for this life, it is as if one is prevented from going forward on the path of *mahamudra*. This is why to be free of this attachment constitutes the legs of the practice.

This non-attachment proceeds from an understanding of the nature of all phenomena. In the state of non-realization, all phenomena and external objects such as forms, sounds, smells, and so on, as well as our body and the internal appearances produced in our mind, are all apprehended as endowed with a real and permanent existence. This is a mistaken apprehension.

On the contrary, one must be conscious that the external phenomena which our senses perceive, far from being endowed with this permanence we attribute to them, are transitory; they are modified from instant to instant. Our body and mind are submitted to the same processes of constant modification.

Let us take, for example, the house in which we find ourselves. It is apparently the same as yesterday, the same as last year. It seems that nothing has changed. This is only a false impression. At the imperceptible level of the molecules which constitute the building, continual change is occurring such that it never remains the same. A new house does not continue to be new on account of this constant modification. This change determines its aging and ensures that a day will come when it is only a ruin, and it will finally disappear completely. This is true for everything, even things that appear the most durable, such as mountains or rocks. Everything is impermanent.

Our body and our mind do not escape this law. I consider for instance, that today I am Bokar Tulku, that yesterday I was Bokar Tulku, that last year I was also Bokar Tulku. I might have the tendency to think that I am always the same Bokar Tulku. However, my body changes from instant to instant, as does my mind[1] which is no longer the same as it was in the past.

To this understanding of impermanence must be added the consciousness of the inherent suffering of the cycle of existence. If we consider only the beings that populate the earth, we can verify a magnitude of continual suffering that afflicts them, physical as well as internal suffering. It sometimes happens that we look happy with no visible suffering but this is not true happiness because it is not definitive and will transform into suffering sooner or later. Even a neutral state, without suffering or happiness, by the nature of the mental dullness that it implies, will also bring about suffering. It is said that three sorts of suffering exist: the suffering of pain, the suffering of change, and the suffering inherent in everything that is composed of elements. This being the case, no being in *samsara* knows a state of genuine happiness.

From the moment we understand that all external and internal phenomena are impermanent, that they are stained by suffering, and that *samsara* is no longer interesting, our attachment to the appearances of this life diminishes. From then on, we can turn toward the methods of liberation that allow us to attain Buddhahood.

THE HEAD: DEVOTION

Devotion is considered to be the head of the practice of *mahamudra*. The object of this devotion is all the *lamas* of the lineage of transmission, and especially, the one that we call *"source lama,"* or the teacher who introduces us directly to the nature of our own mind.

---

[1] *Mind* refers here to the psyche which is changeable. On the other hand, the essence of the mind is immutable.

Devotion is essential because without it one cannot open oneself to grace, and without the latter, realization of *mahamudra* would remain impossible. One often compares the grace of the teacher to a snow-covered mountain and the devotion of the student to the sun whose rays touch the slopes of the mountain. The warmth of the sun melts the snow so we can catch the water and drink it. But if the sun of devotion does not shine the snow will not melt. Thus we will not receive the indispensable grace.

THE BODY: MEDITATION

On one hand, non-attachment to the cycle of existence and the wish to liberate oneself from it, and on the other, devotion, constitute the legs and head of the practice. One could not do without these and still reach the third point: the meditation that contemplates the nature of the mind.

This meditation requires the knowledge of how to "position" the body and how to "position" the mind.

Great importance is accorded to the body's posture, because there is interdependence between our body and mind. A correct body posture will assist in developing stability of mind, whereas an incorrect posture will be detrimental to this stability. Therefore, ideally one takes the posture called the "seven point posture of Vairocana" as mentioned before:

- legs crossed in the *vajra* position;
- hands in the *mudra* of meditation;
- spine straight as an arrow;
- shoulders open like the wings of a vulture;
- chin drawn in slightly;
- tongue placed against the palate in a relaxed way, with relaxed lips;
- eyes gazing into space, angled downwards.

For those who find it difficult to maintain this posture, it can be summarized in two essential points: spinal column perfectly straight and hands in the *mudra* of meditation.

Once the body is well established in this posture, one must learn to settle the mind. How do we learn to do this?

First, one notices that a multitude of thoughts about the past or future arise in our mind. The thoughts of the past may be related to things that occurred several years ago, some months ago, hours ago, or they may relate to what happened just few minutes ago. In the same manner, thoughts of the future can envision events to come in several years, in a few days, a few hours, or in the next minute. With regard to these thoughts of the past or future, one does not follow them. One only rests in the mind, as it is, in the present and without distraction.

Remaining without distraction with the mind in the present is what one calls the meditation of *mahamudra*.

Some people will think that meditating like this, without being caught up in thoughts of past and future, must be extremely difficult, even frightening. However, if the mind ceases to project itself into that which has been, or into that which will be, and rests as it is in the present, open and relaxed, it will have a feeling of rest which makes meditation easy and pleasant.

STILL MIND, MOVING MIND

In this state of relaxation of the body and inner non-distraction, the mind will, for a moment, remain still and without thoughts. Other moments, thoughts will arise, and during that time the mind will be moving. When the mind is still, one recognizes it and rests in this state. When thoughts arise, one recognizes that also in the same manner. The right way to proceed, then, is to avoid two attitudes:

• considering that thoughts are bad and that it is necessary to stop their production;
• following them without being conscious of it.

On the contrary, without either stopping or following them, one remains relaxed in a state of simple recognition.

The meditation of *mahamudra* *is* the mind settled in the present.

When their mind rests calm and stable, beginners tend to rejoice, telling themselves that their meditation is good. At the other extreme, when many thoughts arise, they feel thwarted and discouraged, convinced that they will never be able to meditate. Here again are two mistaken reactions.

Ordinarily, we follow thoughts without even being conscious of them; we are deluded by them. With respect to meditation, there is no implication that we should be afraid of them, wish for their disappearance, or try to stop them. Regarding thoughts, one should remain without rejecting or accepting them. Whether they are there or not is of no importance.

The important point of meditation is not the absence of thoughts, but maintaining a non-distracted vigilance, without judgment, and free of the notions of good or bad.

These, then, are the three parts that comprise a complete and genuine practice of *mahamudra*: the legs of non-attachment, the head of devotion and the trunk of the mind resting in the present, as it is, without distraction, without refusing anything and without accepting anything.

Mahamudra in Five Points

The understanding of the ultimate nature of the mind cannot be achieved through intellectual investigation. It is only attainable through meditation because only meditation leads to direct experience.

The Buddha's words are collected in works classified in two categories the *sutras*[1] and the *tantras*. One can find in them a great variety of approaches to meditation. However, the essence of all these methods, including those in both the *sutras* and *tantras*, is included in what is called the *"mahamudra* in five points."

The five points are:
- *taking Refuge* and developing *bodhicitta;*
- visualizing oneself as the deity;
- praying to the *lama;*
- meditating;
- dedicating the merit [to all beings].

---

[1]The *sutras* can be considered the exoteric teaching of Buddha and the *tantras* his esoteric teachings.

REFUGE AND BODHICITTA

The first point consists of reciting the *Refuge* formula and developing the mind of Awakening, the *bodhicitta*[1], at the beginning of meditation.

Taking Refuge is placing oneself under the protection of the Buddhas, the *dharma* (their teachings) and the *sangha* (those who transmit these teachings after having integrated them internally). This is considered the foundation of the Buddhist path.

We think, then, that numerous Buddhas and *bodhisattvas*[2] reside in the *pure lands*[3] of the *ten directions*[4],

---

[1]Numerous formulas exist which express *taking Refuge* and developing *bodhicitta*. Let us give an example of one of the shortest which is also one of the most common:
Until Awakening, I take Refuge in the Buddha, the Dharma and the sublime Sangha.
By the merit engendered by my practice of giving and the other perfections,
May I realize Awakening for the benefit of all beings.
Or, also:
With all beings, my past mothers
Infinite as space in number,
I take Refuge in my Teacher, the precious Buddha,
I take Refuge in the Buddha, Dharma and Sangha,
I take Refuge in the Masters, Yidams and Dakinis,
I take Refuge in my own mind, emptiness-light, Absolute Body.

[2]*Bodhisattvas*: beings endowed with a very high realization but not yet having attained full Awakening. They are seen as the ideal of the Great Vehicle (*Mahayana*) on the path that leads to Buddhahood because they consecrate themselves totally to benefit suffering beings.

[3]The *pure lands* are domains of manifestation created by different Buddhas and seen as their "residence." They do not belong to *samsara*, are free of suffering, and allow beings of sufficient purity access to them in order to quickly progress toward Awakening.

and we *take Refuge* in them until we obtain Awakening.

Then we develop *bodhicitta*, the root of the Great Vehicle, which is the wish to obtain Awakening not for oneself but in order to become capable of helping all beings. One thinks, "In order to help all beings in all the worlds, I must attain Awakening. It is with this goal in mind that I meditate today."

VISUALIZING ONESELF AS THE DEITY

After having taken *Refuge* and developed *bodhicitta*, one visualizes oneself in the form of a *yidam*, a deity of meditation. If you have a personal *yidam* you become one with it, if not, visualize yourself as Chenrezig[1], for example.

PRAYING TO THE LAMA

When visualizing oneself in the form of Chenrezig, one imagines the Buddha Amitabha above one's head, red in color, with an alms bowl in his hands. One considers that his form is really that of Amitabha, but he is also our own *source lama*, embodying all the Buddhas, the *dharma* and the *sangha*.

One prays to him with an intense fervor: "Bestow your grace so that the realization of the ultimate nature, the *mahamudra*, takes birth in my mind in this life."

---

[4]The *ten directions*: the four cardinal points (north, south, east, and west), the four intermediary ones, the zenith and the nadir.

[1]Chenrezig represents the infinite compassion of all the Buddhas. For more information, refer to *Chenrezig, Lord of Love* (ClearPoint Press).

One then visualizes that the *lama*, in the form of Amitabha, melts into light, and this light is absorbed through the crown of one's head, still considering oneself as Chenrezig. The Body, Speech, and Mind of the *lama* then unite with our body, speech and mind.

MEDITATION

One lets the mind rest in a state of union with the *lama* of the previous prayer.

It is possible that nothing in particular occurs, but it is also possible that one has an inexpressible experience of the nature of the mind. That which is discovered is inexpressible. One is a little like a mute person to whom a sweet is given. When asked, "Is it good?," this person would not be able to answer.

If the experience that we have remains expressible, it means we have not reached the goal. To say that something cannot be expressed does not mean it does not exist. Experience beyond words and concepts truly exists; it is precisely that of the ultimate nature of the mind.

Whether or not one has this experience quickly is of no importance. Through perseverance in meditation, it will occur at some moment, and one will then understand the nature of the mind. Even if it occurs at the very beginning, it will not be continuously maintained. Maybe it will occur again, maybe it will not. One should not, in the second case, think that one's meditation is bad or useless. These are normal stages.

This experience [of *mahamudra*] does not imply any direction given to the mind, any intention, or any support on which to lean.

USING A MEANS OF SUPPORT
Given that, in what we have just envisaged, the

mind is resting in nothing but its own nature, and that the experience occurs only in relation to the mind itself, this meditation may appear to be difficult for beginners.

When this is the case, one can temporarily use a means which allows a progressive approach. This means consists of taking as a support an outer object on which to rest one's mind.

This does not mean that one begins to analyze the object. One examines neither its shape, material composition, different parts, nor its name, and so on. One simply lets one's mind rest on the object without distraction.

If the chosen object is a sound, one does not analyze it either. One does not think: this is the sound of a car, this is the sound of a motorbike, this sound is loud, this one is pleasant, this one unpleasant. One rests in a non-discursive state in which sound and mind are one. Taking sound as a support is very easy for the people who live in a noisy environment. Because integrated into meditation, sound ceases to be an obstacle.

In the same way, one can take smells as supports. Whether they are agreeable or disagreeable, they are perceived without judgment. One can also use tastes, or even objects of touch, disengaging oneself from the notions of good or bad. Whatever the chosen object, mind and object are one without any added concepts.

A secluded place is an ideal environment for the practice. In this case, when the demands of external objects are less numerous, one lets the mind rest in itself. If not, one takes the sense object that is predominant as support: a visual form, a sound, a smell, a taste and so on.

When one is a beginner in meditation, the best way to proceed, is to take external objects as supports, then for short periods, to let the mind rest in itself. One can proceed like this alternatively.

NOT "FOLLOWING" THE THOUGHTS

Thoughts arise when one meditates but it is of no importance. One should not believe that thoughts are bad. Neither does this mean that following thoughts is not a hindrance. In fact, one should neither follow them nor reject them. One should not occupy oneself with them at all, not pay any attention to them. Let us take an example.

(Bokar Rinpoche takes three objects which are on the table in front of him and gives them to three different people. To the first he gives a bell, to the second a small object called a "vajra," and to the third, a glass.)

There you are. In this example, I am, myself, the mind that meditates, having chosen as object the crystal sphere lying on the table.

(Bokar Rinpoche remains with his eyes fixed on the crystal sphere. At the same time, he asks the first person to hold out the bell as if to give it to him. Bokar Rinpoche turns toward the person, becomes interested in the bell, and finally takes it in his hands, examines it and makes it ring.)

If I take my eyes from the sphere to turn toward the bell it is the same as following a thought.

(Bokar Rinpoche then asks the second person to hold out the vajra. But this time he does not turn his eyes away from the sphere and leaves the person with his arm stretched, not looking at him. Finally, he asks the third person to present him with the glass but he pays no attention.)

This time, even if one offers me the *vajra*, then the glass, I pay no attention. I remain with the mind resting on the chosen support for the meditation.

Thoughts are like the objects that you held out to me. Even if presented with a great number of them, I do not turn toward them, and do not take them. It is of no importance. If, on the contrary, when one offers me the bell, I take it, look at it, and start to play with it, I am then taken by the play of thoughts. I am distracted and I do not meditate any longer.

During meditation, one remains with the mind resting on the chosen object without distraction. The thoughts which may arise are without importance.

One often considers the totality of the path as composed of four aspects:
• the "view," that is to say, the correct intellectual understanding;
• the meditation;
• the conduct;
• the fruit.

Of the first two, the view is useful and important, but meditation is much more important. It is meditation which brings us true benefit. Through meditation comes the inner experience from which we derive peace and happiness, and through meditation one can liberate oneself from suffering.

DEDICATION

When we finish meditating, we make a dedication. We wish that the merit, namely all the positive potential stemming from this meditation, will serve to benefit all beings. This will permit us to obtain Awakening in this lifetime for their sake. We also wish that all beings may quickly attain Awakening.

These are, then, the five stages of "*mahamudra* in five points."

These are the direct and profound instructions of the *Kagyupa* lineage.

SMALL GLOSSARY

ACCUMULATION OF MERIT: Practice of positive *acts* allowing us to store energy for the progression on the spiritual path. This accumulation of merit can be done through the practice of giving, making offerings, reciting *mantras*, visualizing deities and so on.

ACCUMULATION OF WISDOM: Practice of understanding the empty nature of all phenomena.

ACT: Physical action as well as words or thoughts.

AMITABHA: *Buddha* of Infinite Light. *Buddha* of the Lotus Family, manifestation of discriminating wisdom.

AWAKENING: State of *Buddhahood.*

BEINGS: There are six classes of *beings*: gods, demigods, human beings, animals, hungry ghosts and hell beings.

BODHICITTA: Aspiration to obtain *Awakening* in order to help all beings.

BODHISATTVA: Being who follows the *bodhicitta* path and seeks to obtain *Awakening* not only for oneself but for the sake of all *beings*. An ordinary being who commits to practice *bodhicitta*. One who has attained *Awakening* and dwells in one of the ten stages of the *bodhisattvas*. A *bodhisattva* can be physically present in our world or abide in domains of more subtle manifestation.

BODHISATTVA POSTURE: Seated with legs crossed, left heel against the perineum, right foot and leg are bent flat in front.

BODY: Ordinary physical *body*. State of possessing numerous qualities, in Sanskrit, *kaya*.

BUDDHA NATURE: Potential of *Awakening* inherent in all *beings*.

BUDDHA: One who has *awakened*. A person, such as the historical *Buddha Sakyamuni*. In Tibetan *Sangyay*. *Sang* means purified from the conflicting emotions, duality and ignorance; *gyay* means that the infinite potential of qualities of a *being* is *awakened*.

BUDDHAHOOD: *Awakened* state characterized by wisdom (as knowledge of the true nature of phenomena and their manifestation in the *three times*), *compassion* for every *being* and power to help all *beings*.

CHENREZIG (Tibetan): Avalokitesvara (Sanskrit). *Buddha of Compassion*. Most popular Tibetan deity, his *mantra* is OM MA NI PAD ME HUNG. See *Chenrezig, Lord of Love* (ClearPoint Press).

COMPASSION: Aspiration to liberate all *beings* from *suffering* and cause of *suffering*.

CONFLICTING EMOTIONS: Desire-attachment, hatred-aversion, ignorance or mental dullness, jealousy, pride and so on.

DEDICATION: Aspiration that any merit accumulated through our positive *acts* serves to attain *Awakening* for the benefit of all *beings*.

DHARMA: *Buddha's* teachings or the spiritual path.

DHARMAKAYA: Absolute Body, designating a state

beyond any spacial or temporal determination; corresponds to emptiness.

DORJE SEMPA (Tibetan): Vajrasattva (Sanskrit), deity of the *Vajrayana* who is the source of *purification* practices. The practice of *Dorje Sempa* includes a *visualization* as well as recitation of a *mantra*.

FIVE POISONS: Desire, anger, ignorance, pride and jealousy.

GURU YOGA: Practice of prayer and meditation in order to unite our mind with the mind of an *Awakened* teacher.

KAGYUPA: One of the four great schools of Tibetan Buddhism. The other ones are Gelugpa, Nyingma and Sakya schools. The *Kagyu* lineage originates with Marpa the Translator in the 11th century.

KARMA: The law of *karma* describes the process of cause and effect. It is a three-phase process;
- an *act* leaves an imprint in the mind of the one who acts (cause).
- this *act* is stored in the potential of consciousness and is slowly ripening.
- this process is actualized in a particular form of *suffering* or joy (result).

LAMA (Tibetan): Guru (Sanskrit). A spiritual teacher.

LHATONG (Tibetan): Vipassana (Sanskrit), superior vision, meditation practice as direct experience of the nature of the mind.

LOVE: Aspiration to bring happiness to all *beings*.

MAHAMUDRA: Literally the "great seal," designates the ultimate nature of the mind as well as the method of meditation to achieve it.

MANDALA: Literally "center and surrounding." The world seen as an organized universe. Designates a deity with its surrounding environment. Can be represented on a *tangka* which is then used as a *support* for the *visualizations*.

MANDALA OFFERING: Practice during which we imagine offering the *mandala* of the universe to the *Buddha, Dharma* and *Sangha*.

MANTRA: Sacred sounds, the repetition of which helps the mind purify itself and develop its potential for *Awakening*. For example, the *mantra* of Chenrezig is OM MA NI PAD ME HUNG.

MIND: This term can refer to the ordinary functioning of the *mind* called "psyche" as well as the absolute, non-dual pure essence of the *mind* beyond the fluctuations that may affect the ordinary mind.

MODE OF BEING OF THE MIND: Nature of the *mind*. *Buddha nature*.

MUDRA: Hand gesture done during rituals.

NIRMANAKAYA: *Body* of Emanation; appears as human or other forms to guide ordinary *beings*.

NIRVANA: Literally extinguished, cessation. Early definition included liberation from conditioned existence, ignorance and conflicting emotions. Later definitions were expanded to include the development of great *compassion* through skillful means.

OBSCURATION: Conflicting emotions and dualistic perception that veil our *Buddha nature*.

OBSTACLES: Circumstances not favorable to the *dharma* practice which can be experienced as external *obstacles*, internal *obstacles* (sickness) and secret *obstacles* (our own thoughts).

PURE LAND: Domain of manifestation of a *Buddha's mind*. There are many *Pure Lands* one can access depending on one's aspiration and accomplishment. They are not part of *samsara* and are not affected by *suffering*. Being born there does not mean that one has achieved complete *Awakening* but will provide one with the means to progress on the spiritual path. For example, Dewachen is *Amitabha's Pure Land*.

PURE SUPPORTS: They are used in meditation. Statues representing the *Buddha's* body; Texts expressing the *Buddha's* speech; *stupas* symbolizing the *Buddha's* mind.

PURIFICATION: All negative *acts* done in this life and in the past lives have left imprints in our potential of consciousness. These imprints will ripen, engendering *suffering* and *obstacles* to our spiritual practice. *Purification* will neutralize these imprints in order to avoid or reduce their effects. A qualified teacher might designate specific practice to do in order to purify oneself.

SAKYAMUNI: Literally "wise man of the Sakya," name of the historical *Buddha* who lived in the 6th century BC.

SAMBHOGAKAYA: *Body* of Perfect Experience, it appears to guide beings in the *Pure Lands*.

SAMSARA: Cycle of conditioned existence in which each

being is born and dies. It is characterized by *suffering*, ignorance, impermanence and illusion.

SANGHA: Community of Buddhist practitioners. One distinguishes ordinary *sangha* from the Noble *Sangha* which is composed of those who have attained the *bodhisattva* levels.

SHINAY (tibetan): Shamatha (Sanskrit). Mental calming. Meditation practice which frees the *mind* from reacting to the play of thoughts. It can be done with or without *support*.

SOURCE LAMA: Generally, the *lama* we recognize as "our" teacher, who gives us initiations, instructions to practice and explanation of the texts. More particularly, the *lama* who allows us to directly experience the true nature of the *mind*.

STUPA: Monument or sacred object symbolizing the *mind* of the *Buddhas* and which spreads their spiritual energies.

SUBTLE WINDS: Prana (Sanskrit). Winds or energies which circulate in the *subtle channels* and link the *body* to the *mind*.

SUBTLE CHANNELS: Nadis (Sanskrit). Network of invisible channels through which circulate the *subtle winds* or prana.

SUFFERING: Generally it is analyzed on three levels.
- *suffering* of *suffering*: physical and mental pain experienced by all *beings*.
- *suffering* of change: one experiences *suffering* when happiness ends.
- *suffering* of conditioned existence is suffering one undergoes because of the deluded nature of *samsara*. It ends

only when one attains *Awakening*.

SUFFERING OF THE HUMAN REALM: Birth, aging, sickness, death, sorrow, grief, despair, getting things we do not like, loosing things we like, not getting what we wish for, and so on.

SUPPORT: Any object of concentration, material or mental used by a practitioner in meditation.

SUTRA (Sanskrit): Text of the exoteric teachings of the *Buddha*.

SVABHAVIKAKAYA: *Body* of Essence Itself, unity of the three first Bodies (Dharmakaya, Nirmanakaya and Sambhogakaya).

TAKING REFUGE: Placing oneself under the protection of the *Buddha, Dharma* and *Sangha* (the Three Jewels). In the *Vajrayana*, one takes also *Refuge* in the Three Roots, *lamas, yidams* and dharma protectors.

TANGKA (Tibetan): Traditional painting on cloth representing deities, *mandalas* or teachers of the lineage.

TANTRA: Text of the esoteric teachings of the *Buddha* which is related to a deity.

TEN DIRECTIONS: North, South, East, West, four intermediate positions, zenith and nadir.

THREE TIMES: The past, present and future.

TIGLE (Tibetan): Bindu (Sanskrit). Small sphere of light visualized during meditation.

VAIROCANA POSTURE: It is also called seven-point posture: 1. legs in vajra position, 2. hands in meditation *mudra*, 3. straight spine, 4. open shoulders, 5. chin down, 6. eyes gazing in space downward and 7. relaxed tongue.

VAJRA: Ritual object used with a bell. Diamond which symbolizes the indestructible purity of the nature of the mind. The deity *Dorje Sempa* holds a *vajra* in his right hand. See cover of the book.

VAJRA POSTURE: It is also called "diamond posture". Seated with legs crossed, first, the left foot on the right thigh and the right foot on the left thigh.

VAJRAYANA: Path of Buddhism also called "Diamond vehicle" referring to the part of the *Buddha's* teachings written in texts of an esoteric nature called *tantras*. It uses recitation of *mantras, visualizations* of deities and works with the *subtle winds* or energies.

VEILS: That which obscures our *Buddha nature* such as ignorance, latent conditioning, dualistic perception, *conflicting emotion, karmic* veils and so on.

VISUALIZATION: Creation of a mental image used as a support in a meditation or ritual. These images can be geometrical forms or deities, moving or still. This exercise is not dependant upon visual perception but upon inner faculty of imagining.

YIDAM: A personal deity expressing the pure nature of the *mind*. A deity upon which one meditates after having received an initiation.

INDEX

OBSCURATION, 60
OBSTACLES, 17, 29, 32, 60, 72, 78, 137
PURE LAND, 134
PURIFICATION, 25, 60, 63
REFUGE, 28, 29, 60, 63, 109, 110, 111, 114, 126, 129, 134, 139
SAKYAMUNI, 12, 78, 115
SAMBHOGAKAYA, 12
SAMSARA, 27, 28, 37, 48, 60, 73, 126, 129, 134
SANGHA, 134, 135
SHINAY, 7, 9, 59, 68, 70, 73, 76, 78, 79, 81, 82, 85-87, 98-101,
106, 110, 111, 114-116, 119, 120, 121, 125
SOURCE LAMA, 127, 129, 135
SUBTLE CHANNEL, 5, 66
SUBTLE WIND, 6, 66, 76
SUPPORT, 12, 32, 33, 39, 61, 68, 70, 77, 78, 83, 86, 115, 118,
126, 136, 137, 138
SUTRA, 133
SVABHAVIKAKAYA, 12
TANGKA, 115
TANTRA, 133
TEN DIRECTIONS, 134
THREE TIMES, 13
TIGLE, 70, 77, 83, 84, 85, 115
VAIROCANA POSTURE, 77, 130
VAJRA, 138
VAJRA POSTURE, 76, 130
VAJRAYANA, 60, 63, 74
VISUALIZATION, 63, 70, 78, 84, 86, 109, 120
YIDAM, 134, 135